What Can I Bring?

By Debbie Crosby with photography by Bob Crosby

Kindle Direct Publishing©2021

ISBN: 979-8-7086-3866-3

 Some of these photos and more are available at: https://www.istockphoto.com/portfolio/bobwc?assettype=image&mediatype=photography&sort=mostpopular

Table of Contents

Dedication

This Offering is dedicated to God

With deep gratitude for the Joy of knowing His Love and experiencing His Presence!

To our children, Michael and Stephanie, son-in-law Josh, and grandkids Evelyn and Bennett; we love you and are so grateful for each one of you! Thank you for all the ways you continually enrich and bless our lives!

Also, to the memory of Kimberly Blair; with a special note of thanks to her parents Jim and Marilyn, and her brother Craig, for sharing Kimberly with us. In her quiet, brilliant way Kimberly brightened the world with the light of Jesus; teaching those of us lucky enough to spend time with her what the face of love, faith and trust looks like; and what a beautiful impact these treasures can have in a world that needs them so! I have no idea how things work in Heaven, but perhaps God would convey this message for us. Dearest Kimberly, you were an angel to so many then and we rejoice knowing you are an angel now, completely unconstrained and glorious! Thank God for you and eternity!

Kimberly's photo taken by her mother, Marilyn Blair

With Gratitude for and Special Thanks to:

All my Pastors past and present who have helped me on my journey; notably Pastors Christian Pye and Luke Bushman of Hammond Bay Baptist Church, Nanaimo, British Columbia.; Pastors Jeff Edwards, and Kara Wilfley of Northwest Community Church, Calgary, Alberta; Pastor Ken Peters of Saanich Community Church, Saanich, British Columbia; and Pastor Aaron Dyck of Gateway Baptist Church, Victoria, British Columbia. You all serve faithfully and authentically and I'm grateful for your teaching, service and friendship! Thanks also to Pastors Lindsay Anderson, Eric West, David Horita, Paul Olson and Steve Laug. I'm thankful for your faith filled lessons and trust you are still blessing God's "flock!"

My believing "family" young and old, who meet, teach, learn, serve and encourage us all. Special thanks to the youth at Northwest Community Church in Calgary Alberta, who, one cool Advent morning asked; "What will you bring the King next year?" It took me more than a year but the early drafts were finished in twelve months and what a blessing this journey has been! A huge thank you for igniting the conviction and prayer that led to this book!

The precious women in my life, who, like Jesus, have met me where I'm at and loved me in spite of myself; have listened, prayed, shared, taught and mentored me on this most wonderful, challenging journey towards our Heavenly Home! Since I don't trust my sometimes scattered brain and may unintentionally leave someone out, I will avoid putting your names in print though I would dearly love to! I trust you know who you are. I would though, like to make special mention of two ladies who, when I was a very new Christian, led me in Bible studies and took special care to guide me on my way; providing godly wisdom with great humility, acceptance and compassion: Lillian Scott and Rachel Workman started me on a journey that changed my life; as did the gift of a generous stranger; one Clarence Roskamp of Covenant Presbyterian Church in Cedar Falls, Iowa, who donated an NIV Bible that brought the Word of God to life for me! Mr. Roskamp, I don't know if you'll ever see this but Rachel passed your gift along to me and I always wished I could thank you! It has been such a blessing!

Last but by no means least, to my dear friends; Adrianne Haynes and Marilyn Blair; thank you for previewing this and providing valuable insights and suggestions; and especially to my husband Bob for the sampling of your stunning photography and much needed technical assistance! Our forty one years together have seen their share of troubles but they have also been rich in love and life experiences. Thank you for choosing to love me and honour our vows these many years! The good and the hard times have shaped who we are becoming and have brought us closer to God and each other. In John 10:10 God tells us "The thief comes only to steal and kill and destroy; I have come that they may have life, and have it to the full." Praise God that "for better or worse, for richer or poorer, in sickness and in health," our lives are indeed "full" and we have so much to be thankful for!

Introduction

"I have told you these things, so that in me you may have peace. In this world you will have trouble. But take heart! I have overcome the world." (John 16:33)

This book was born of a heartfelt challenge by a group of young people, plenty of prayer and a deep desire to serve God. We've all had our share of troubles. Mine are no greater than yours. Neither am I an expert on the Word of God but I have met with Him through many life challenges and hope that by sharing some of these experiences I might honour God and help others who struggle.

Have you ever noticed that when we step out to do something for another, it often seems as if the blessing we receive is far greater than that of our recipient's? It's strange really that the more we try to bless others the more we receive. That has certainly been the case with this offering. I set out to answer a question and bring a gift to my King, but in the end it was another of His many gifts to me. I hope it will be a gift for you too.

By God's grace and to His glory may the pages that follow help you to see God's hand in your circumstances; and to seek your comfort, peace and ultimate joy from the only One who can truly offer up such gifts; our Divine Saviour Jesus Christ! God Bless You on your journey!

"But blessed is the one who trusts in the LORD, whose confidence is in Him. They will be like a tree planted by the water that sends out its roots by the stream. It does not fear when heat comes; its leaves are always green. It has no worries in a year of drought and never fails to bear fruit." (Jeremiah 17:7-8)

Cover Photo: Lake Wakatipu, Queenstown, New Zealand. © Bob Crosby

When We Suffer – God as Our Provider

Canary Hot Spring, Yellowstone National Park, U.S.A. © Bob Crosby

This other worldly spectacle is located in the remnants of the "super volcano" we now call Yellowstone Park. The land was ripped away by a violent explosion around 640,000 years ago shooting ash skyward and forming a giant caldera. Today the land is still wild and seismically active. The staff at Yellowstone National Park explain how waters that flow underground in some of the hot springs, like this one in Mammoth Hot Springs, become charged with carbon dioxide and form a mild carbonic acid. The acid eats away at the limestone rocks below the surface. Then the carbon dioxide that initially did the damage comes to the aid of the dissolved limestone helping the water to carry it to the surface. There the dissolved particles knit together to become a solid formation once more, only this time spreading out to form exquisite travertine terraces for so many to enjoy.

This stunning view reminds me of how even devastating circumstances can become a space for positive change and beauty to grow. In John 11:35 we learn "Jesus wept" for his friend Lazarus. Why did He weep when he knew that Lazarus would be raised from the dead? I don't know but I believe God's love for us is so great that He feels our anguish, and weeps with us when we suffer. When every little particle of our being seems to be dissolving, He weeps; but then He gets on to the business of moving us on and making our outcome beautiful.

In a world that can be cold, hard and unforgiving God is still there; He loves us, anchors us, forgives us and allows our pain to become something beautiful as it blesses others.

"The heavens declare the glory of God; the skies proclaim the work of his hands. Day after day they pour forth speech; night after night they display knowledge. There is no speech or language where their voice is not heard. Their voice goes out into all the earth, their words to the ends of the world.

In the heavens He has pitched a tent for the sun, which is like a bridegroom coming forth from his pavilion, like a champion rejoicing to run his course. It rises at one end of the heavens and makes its circuit to the other; nothing is hidden from its heat.

The law of the Lord is perfect, reviving the soul. The statutes of the Lord are right, giving joy to the heart. The commands of the Lord are radiant, giving light to the eyes. The fear of the Lord is pure, enduring forever. The ordinances of the Lord are sure and altogether righteous. They are more precious than gold, than much pure gold; they are sweeter than honey, than honey from the comb. By them is your servant warmed; in keeping them there is great reward.

Who can discern his errors? Forgive my hidden faults. Keep your servant also from willful sins; may they not rule over me. Then will I be blameless, innocent of great transgression.

May the words of my mouth and the meditation of my heart be pleasing in your sight, O Lord, my Rock and my Redeemer." (Psalm 19)

As God created our world, He filled it with all the building blocks of science, brilliantly arranged to gift us here on Earth. One by one, he gave us a world filled with everything we'd need for our survival; intricately designed to work together for our good. Along with the practicalities God provided, He also gave graciously of His glorious beauty and breathtaking wonders.

Reflecting on God's gifts, it seems to me they are a grand display of something God models and allows us to do for others; only in our case, on a much smaller scale. When others are hurting we are called to provide practically; food, warmth or whatever else is needed. Then, just as God does for us over and over again, we can add some sparkle to our gift; something that is extravagant in its lack of purpose; a beautiful flower hand-picked from our garden, a smile or a hug to brighten one's day; something to say *'you're not alone. I'm here for you.'*

Isn't that what God does every moment of our days? It seems wise to remember and let our hearts soar, much like King David the Psalmist, remembering all the goodness that surrounds us thanks to our Heavenly Father, Precious Saviour Jesus and the ever present Holy Spirit guiding us on this earthly journey. We can receive God's gifts with gratitude and share with joy.

As God worked towards His provision for us, He looked on what He had made and "saw that it was good." Then when he "created the great creatures of the sea and every living and moving thing with which the water teems, according to their kinds and every winged bird according to its kind," He not only " saw that it was good." God also "blessed them and said, "Be fruitful and increase in number."(Genesis 1: 21-22)

That blessing was just for "the creatures of the sea and every winged bird." His crowning glory was reserved for man; "Then God said, 'Let us make man in our image, in our likeness, and let them rule over the fish of the sea and the birds of the air, over the livestock, over all the earth and over all the creatures that move along the ground.' So God created man in his own image, in the image of God he created him, male and female he created them. God blessed them and said to them, 'Be fruitful and increase in number, fill the earth and subdue it. Rule over the fish of the sea and the birds of the air and over every living creature that moves on the ground.' " (Genesis 1: 26-28)

God not only provided everything we would need, He also gave us stewardship over it all. It was for us to respect, care for, harvest and renew, as guided by Him. It's good to be guided by our God; a God who blesses even the smallest "fish of the sea and birds of the air."

When I'm feeling small, alone, afraid or discouraged, it's comforting to think that He loves all His creatures and blesses us so graciously, even if at the time it is hard to fathom. Let's face it; there are times that don't feel much like blessings! They can test one's faith especially when we or those we love are suffering, but we can still turn to God.

"Praise be to the God and Father of our Lord Jesus Christ, the Father of compassion and the God of all comfort, who comforts us in all our troubles, so that we can comfort those in any trouble with the comfort we ourselves receive from God."(2nd Corinthians 1:3-4) There it is again; we receive and then we share. God provides and equips so that we can bless others.

So, where is God when we suffer? I have a significant number of non-believers in my life. It breaks my heart but I get where they are coming from. At the root of virtually all their protests is the issue of suffering; the age old – if God is all powerful and all loving why doesn't He take my pain/ the world's pain away?

I don't have an answer that satisfies my loved ones. That one word; "faith" seems weak to the world. They can't see God's bigger picture and I'm at a loss to show them. I can't see it either! Faith is just that, believing without seeing. "Now faith is confidence in what we hope for and assurance about what we do not see." (Hebrews 11.1) Still, with all my heart and mind, I believe that centuries ago God took away our pain when it was nailed to the cross, and He continues to do so, just not always in the way we pray for.

What I do know that bolsters my faith in times of questioning are three things.

First, God is the master sufferer. He sent His only Son knowing full well what He would endure on the cross. Jesus prayed that if it were possible God would take that agony from Him "Father, if you are willing, take this cup from me; yet not my will but yours be done."(Luke 22: 42) His anguish was palpable as Jesus wept in the garden of Gethsemane but He still willingly gave Himself over to the cross. Jesus' love and faith in His Holy Father won over His human fear.

The Holy Spirit lives within each and every soul who has accepted Jesus Christ as Saviour. He never leaves, even if we turn from Him. He is with us every time we're frightened and every time we falter and sin. I wonder if seeing His children in acts of disobedience is as excruciating to Him as the pain was when the nails were driven in and He hung on the cross to pay our debt in full. Knowing that sin is unbearable to God, I can only begin to imagine the suffering we inflict on our God each time we turn away from Him. God Himself suffers for His children.

Secondly, pain is a gift that alerts us to our need for help. It is a by-product of free will, lovingly wrapped up and given to His children. Were it not for pain and suffering we wouldn't learn, know or grow. Sometimes I don't want free will. I want everything to be beautiful, peaceful and joyful. I don't want to face my ugly heart and mind; the part of me that can be so critical and judgemental, vocally or silently berating people I love. Maybe, like me you've had too much to say or think about another or find it too easy while driving down the highway to enthusiastically note the "sins" of the other drivers. How often I've prayed "God please take my thoughts captive! Let them be your thoughts not mine;" instead of praying "God this is your child who you created. Let me see him (or her) through your eyes!" Not that the first prayer isn't valuable, but the thing is that there has never been a time I prayed that alternative prayer that God didn't work miraculously to fulfill it.

I remember a social situation I was dreading that I couldn't get out of. I was not fond of the husband we were going to be visiting and had a whole litany of undeclared complaints against him. Talk about the pot calling the kettle black! I was a pretty new Christian at the time and fortunately God had put a beautiful friend/ spiritual mentor named Rachel into my life. God provides! At a Bible study group a few days before the dreaded meeting we had been talking about challenging relationships. Rachel had spoken up – not intending it for me but it was definitely for me – and explained how she would ask God to help her see difficult people through His eyes." The lightbulb came on. A simple prayer made a huge difference! We had a wonderful visit, I saw a kind and giving side of this man I had never seen before and was filled with genuine godly love for him. It was also very humbling. As with pretty much all the times when I've been critical, God showed me the size of the log in my own eye! "How can you say to your brother, 'Let me take the speck out of your eye,' when all the time there is a plank in your own eye? You hypocrite, first take the plank out of your own eye and then you will see clearly to remove the speck from your brother's eye." (Matthew 7: 4-5) I love the way He corrects me – always lovingly and without shame. If you are experiencing shame you are not experiencing God. Wrap it up and give it to Him and watch what He will do with you. God will always provide exactly what you need.

Thirdly, I trust God's promise "that in all things God works for the good of those who love him, who have been called according to his purpose" (Romans 8:28) even when it doesn't feel that way at the time.

Think about the times when you've been at your very lowest; maybe you're there now. I once spent a number of months suffering from Lyme disease. With that came not just the physiological symptoms. I was depressed; worried that I was losing my mind in the months that it went undiagnosed and untreated and wondered if God was punishing me. I even spent time praying God would just end my life. I'm glad He didn't answer that prayer!

Out of that time period came a host of blessings that I can see now but couldn't see at the time. I had been working full time until I fell ill. My mom had passed away a couple of years earlier and my widowed dad had moved to Victoria to be closer to his daughters. It broke my heart to not be strong enough to spend time with him every day, but I could talk to him on the phone daily and because I wasn't working full time, I could visit when I was able. When Dad landed in hospital I had more time to spend at his bedside, just listening, talking or being together in silence. Dad got better long enough to see his daughter healed thanks again to God's provision – but more on that later - and for us to have a couple of more good years together. I didn't go back to my full time job and so I was again freer to take him to appointments and enjoy more time together.

Today if you asked me if I would rather God had kept that diseased little tick off my leg, my first answer would be of course but in contemplation I would struggle with that answer. My suffering helped Dad in his emotional suffering with loneliness and during his physical suffering too. Meanwhile, Dad was encouraging me. By just spending time and being there with him we supported each other. That time with Dad was such a blessing!

Two years later, Dad took a fall and was back in hospital. As the days progressed he improved. Dad enjoyed his walks with the physiotherapists and would often make the staff or visitors smile when he'd quip "Off we go like a herd of turtles." One nurse even taught me something new. "It's a "bale of turtles, not a herd." It didn't matter; Dad's warmth and sense of humour brightened those halls as much as it cheered him.

One morning the nurses called with bad news. Dad was unresponsive. It was time to call my siblings to his bedside. I spent that day and the night before they arrived in Dad's room with him. While I was praying in the wee hours of the morning I had an overwhelming thought that came spilling out; Oh Lord, it would be so wonderful if Dad would wake up and we could all talk to him again! I know You could do this; please wake him up!" With that I fell back to sleep. A few hours later, Dad suddenly rolled over in his bed, grabbed the rails to pull himself up into a half sitting position, looked over at me and asked "What time is it?" just as if nothing had happened.

"It's 7:30 Dad. Did you have a good rest?"

His enthusiastic response to that; "Did I ever!"

I ran for the nurse to let her know the good news. A short while later, my sister Vikki arrived from the airport and my brother Gord arrived from across the country later that day. Laurie also made it in. We were blessed to be able to be together to support him and each other. My memory is hazy now but I think Dad was with us at least another day, maybe two. We were all with him when he passed at the age of 90. It was a beautiful death! Up until that point I didn't know death could be so beautiful. Our dad loved three things the most in this world – his family, music and laughter. God's "Bon Voyage" gift to him came with all three. As we gathered around his bedside, we started singing some of Dad's favourite hymns and songs. Dad was smiling. None of us are particularly great singers and Gord quipped "Dad you're just smiling because you don't have to listen to us much longer." Our dad got the biggest grin on his face, a beautiful twinkle in his eye and with that he departed.

Dad was a musician and would always end his sets with an old song "We'll meet again, don't know where, don't know when, but I know we'll meet again some sunny day." I'm so grateful that thanks to Christ's gift on that cross, we will!

Holy Father,

Thank You that You never waste our suffering but promise to use it for something good and turn it into something beautiful. Please help us remember that when we're in the midst of it all. Please help us remember too that You have promised "blessed are those who mourn for they will be comforted." (Matthew 5:4) Lord please be our constant comforter in all of our times of sorrow and please don't let us lose sight of the truth that eventually all our pain and sadness will be gone to be replaced by your pure love, peace and joy!

In Jesus Name I pray.

Amen.

What is Love? - God is Our Love

Okanagan Sunset, British Columbia © Bob Crosby

The sunset hour; the time that signals this day is finished. I remember an earlier time, before I was born, when Jesus, hanging on the cross to pay for our sins, declared "It is finished!" And it was. Death was defeated, our sins were cleansed and we became free to dwell with God eternally in this life and the next, free to pray and call out to Him, free to love and forgive with abandon.

We could still choose to stand stubbornly rooted in the muck or weeds of ego, self –entitlement and preconceived notions of ourselves and others if we want to, or we can choose to let God transplant us to His ideal mount for our lives, filled with SON- light and bedded into His nutrient rich love. We are free to loosen the roots that were choking us and relocate if we desire. "Ask and it will be given to you."

All we need to do is reach up and out to God and the others he brings into our lives; and let our Giver nourish us from above with His gifts of love, peace, hope and joy. Accepting God's love and sharing it with others is one of the best ways to show Him our love! Will you stretch your branches towards Him? Will you stretch your branches to others? He's waiting for us all.

“If I speak in the tongues of men and of angels but have not love, I am only a resounding gong or a clanging cymbal. If I have the gift of prophecy and can fathom all mysteries and all knowledge, and if I have a faith that can move mountains, but have not love, I am nothing. If I give all I possess to the poor and surrender my body to the flames, but have not love, I gain nothing.

Love is patient, love is kind. It does not envy, it does not boast, it is not proud. It is not rude, it is not self-seeking, it is not easily angered, it keeps no record of wrongs. Love does not delight in evil but rejoices with the truth. It always protects, always trusts, always hopes, always perseveres.” (1 Corinthians 13:1-7)

I have a tendency to read this passage and see it as a model for how we as humans should live our lives and love others. Suddenly it occurred to me that this isn’t just about how we should be; this is also about how God is! God is love; He is patient, kind, and joyful in our victories. God remained humble when He walked on this earth, was never rude, never self-seeking, and not easily angered. Jesus is forgiving - and forgetting of our failings, delighting and rejoicing in all that is good and true, always there to protect us, always trusting, always hoping and always persevering to save our souls! What a beautiful place to dwell, remembering all He is towards us!

“Jesus said: ‘A man was going down from Jerusalem to Jericho, when he was attacked by robbers. They stripped him of his clothes, beat him and went away, leaving him half dead. A priest happened to be going down the same road, and when he saw the man, he passed by on the other side. So too, a Levite, when he came to the place and saw him, passed by on the other side. But a Samaritan, as he traveled, came where the man was; and when he saw him, he took pity on him. He went to him and bandaged his wounds, pouring on oil and wine. Then he put the man on his own donkey, brought him to an inn and took care of him. The next day he took out two denarii and gave them to the innkeeper. ‘Look after him,’ he said, ‘and when I return, I will reimburse you for any extra expense you may have.’ ” (Luke 10:30-35)

How do we adequately love; Love God? Love our family and our friends? Love our neighbours as ourselves? How can we possibly live up to the Biblical standard and be more like Him in our relationships towards others? What does our love look like?

As I write this we are in the midst of all things Christmas; the season of our celebration of that time over 2000 years ago when LOVE came down to dwell with us.

Yesterday was the last day of school for millions of children, all bright eyed and filled with joy. Except for the ones who weren’t; kids who through no fault of their own are ghostly shells filled with the effects of poverty or abuse. Santa won’t be visiting them in a couple of days unless they are paid a visit by one of the thousands of charities across the country that started because their dedicated volunteers know what love looks like. They have lovingly collected toys and gifts donated by more fortunate “good Samaritans” who also felt the love and wanted to brighten the life of a stranger.

Over and over again Jesus showed us what love looks like. While he demonstrated His love frequently to the people he knew He also made it clear that sacrificial love towards strangers was the pinnacle of love.

The Good Samaritan was a parable, a fictional story meant to teach. Though made up, it created a vivid picture of how to love a stranger. When he knelt to assist the brutally beaten stranger in the street, he didn't know the outcome. He might have just as easily been thinking: *That stranger could die in my company. Wait a minute; I could be accused of his death! After all I'm a Samaritan, nothing more than scum to the Israelites. Maybe he wouldn't even want my help. Let his own people help him. Anyway, I'm so very busy, I don't have time for this, and I certainly don't want to spend my personal resources paying for some ungrateful, scornful stranger...*

One can imagine what might have gone through the Samaritan's head and a completely different outcome for this beloved story! Yet, God's love, the love that He asks of us, was present. "On one occasion an expert in the law stood up to test Jesus. "Teacher," he asked, "what must I do to inherit eternal life?"

"What is written in the Law?" he replied. "How do you read it?"

He answered, "Love the Lord your God with all your heart and with all your soul and with all your strength and with all your mind;" and, "Love your neighbor as yourself."

"You have answered correctly," Jesus replied. "Do this and you will live." (Luke 10: 25-28)

This was the kind of love that would move any "Samaritan" to serve generously; to nurse the stranger's wounds, put him up at an inn and pay out of his own pocket so the stranger would be taken care of. Our Saviour modelled that kind of compassion, care, love and devotion to God and us.

Jesus gave so many examples of His love for us. In John 13, He "got up from the meal, took off his outer clothing, and wrapped a towel around his waist. After that, he poured water into a basin and began to wash his disciples' feet, drying them with the towel that was wrapped around Him... When He had finished washing their feet, He put on his clothes and returned to his place. "Do you understand what I have done for you?" He asked them. You call me 'Teacher' and 'Lord,' and rightly so, for that is what I am. Now that I, your Lord and Teacher have washed your feet, you also should wash one another's feet. I have set you an example that you should do as I have done for you." (John 13:1-15)

Love expressed as a sentiment is beautiful; love expressed in action is divine. In today's world we read and hear a lot about all the reasons we don't need to help strangers. *They'll just spend it on drugs and alcohol. Homeless people choose to live on the street; they wouldn't want housing even if you gave it to them. Let them go out and get a job like everyone else.* Though it is possible there may be a tiny minority of people who these statements would be true of, there are so many more who have been victims of circumstance, economic recession and job loss, mental illness and government shut downs of institutions where they had previously been cared for. I once read about a social study where the author went out into the street to meet the strangers that we too often choose to make invisible. With him he carried alcohol, cigarettes and food. The strangers were given a choice and the vast majority gratefully accepted the food. What if they had chosen the alcohol or cigarettes? Should we not still love those suffering from addictions? I think Jesus would and I believe He would want us to do the same!

We should never allow our preconceived notions to interfere with an opportunity to love. Loving others is a crucial component of loving God. He very clearly tells us "Do not judge, or you too will be judged. For in the same way you judge others, you will be judged, and with the measure you use, it will be measured to you."(Matthew 7:1-2) What's it to us how the person who receives a gift chooses to use that gift? What really matters is the answer to the question: Am I loving the other the way God wants me to? Am I / are we right with God? If the Bible is to be considered, individually and collectively people and nations are held accountable for sins committed against God and others. It's a sobering thought.

I'm no angel and loving others in a sacrificial way is often a struggle. Sometimes it's easier to love a stranger, hand them some money, listen to their story, say a kind word and depart. Loving the difficult colleague or acquaintances – or especially my closest loved ones; my spouse and my kids, can be difficult depending on the day and the situation. Sometimes I don't feel like loving. Sometimes I want to wallow in the mud and muck, indulging my own personal sense of truth and what I view as *their injustice*. Arguing with God; *but Lord don't I deserve respect and goodness too! I know you want me to love and forgive them as you have done for me, but it's just not fair*! I become a foot stomping toddler again demanding what I want from my Father in Heaven. But He just smiles down at me patiently until I come around, and I ask His forgiveness and the grace to love the others as myself. Then He gently reminds me "My yoke is easy and my burden light," (Matthew 11:30) and I remember that the only reason it is a struggle is because I'm trying to do it on my own strength. Miraculously, when I'm willing to give it up, pray and ask the Holy Spirit to take over, the anger, frustration and hurt dissolve. Even though the circumstances haven't changed, I am left with a profound sense of God's love for me and the others and joy even when the bruise still hurts.

Bruises fade but not all wounds disappear. There are scars at times that will never leave us but they can and will be precious reminders of God's provision, mercy and grace if we let them. There are also situations where people are so brutally abused that they absolutely must leave the other and keep as far away from them as possible for their own safety and in many cases for the safety of their children. There is a vast difference between differences of opinion or hurt feelings and physical, mental and emotional abuse. God never asks anyone to endure abuse! I knew a lady whose abusive husband liked to quote "Wives submit to your husband as to the Lord." (Ephesians 5:22) This passage is NOT God giving permission for husbands to abuse their wives! Read the rest of that passage. He spends far more time telling the husbands to love their wives and describing what that looks like; “Husbands, love your wives, even as Christ also loved the church, and gave himself up for her to make her holy, cleansing her by the washing with water through the word and to present her to himself as a radiant church, without stain or wrinkle or any other blemish, but holy and blameless. In this same way, husbands ought to love their wives as their own bodies. He who loves his wife loves himself. After all, no one ever hated his own body, but he feeds and cares for it, just as Christ does the church – for we are members of his body. “For this reason a man will leave his father and mother and be united to his wife, and the two will become one flesh.” (Ephesians 5: 25 – 31)

We should submit only to godly leadership given with love! God tells us “Do you not know that your bodies are temples of the Holy Spirit, who is in you, whom you have received from God? You are not your own, you were bought at a price. Therefore honour God with your body.” (1Corinthians 6:19 -20) Our bodies are His “temple.” Neither men nor women are meant to submit to cruelty; that would never honour God! Sometimes the most loving thing we can do is walk away, saving and protecting ourselves and our children so we can all effectively serve God and society. Sometimes in so doing, we can also help the other come to the place where he or she can seek the help they need to prevent them from committing such atrocities. We can and should leave anyone who is putting our lives in peril but we can and must still forgive from a distance. God taught us to pray “…forgive us our trespasses as we forgive those who trespass against us.”(Matthew 6: 12) These are the predators that are so difficult and often seemingly impossible to forgive “but with God all things are possible.”” (Matthew 19:26) We need to trust Him enough to let go and allow Him to give us the strength we need to do the impossible.

Corrie Ten Boom told just such a story of God’s possibilities when after giving a talk, she was approached by one of her former guards at the concentration camp where she and her sister were sent for harbouring Jews and where her sister Betsie died. The guard had been very cruel but had since become a Christian. He knew God forgave him but he wanted Corrie to forgive him too.

Corrie described that she couldn’t accept his outstretched hand and she couldn’t forgive him, but as she struggled with her thoughts she knew she had no choice. “If you do not forgive men their trespasses,” Jesus says, “neither will your Father in heaven forgive your trespasses.” (Matthew 6:15) Her only choice was to forgive, her only means by prayer and through God’s power.

Praying for help and fighting her demons, Corrie reached out and took his hand. Suddenly, miraculously the forgiveness was there, filling her with warmth and a profound sense of God’s love.

I didn’t know about Corrie ten Boom until I was an adult. A dear lady Ann Penner, who is with the Lord now, invited us into her home every week for Bible studies. At one such gathering she pulled out a tape of an interview with Corrie ten Boom describing her experience. I may have the quote wrong after many years but what I remembered was Corrie saying that in the moment when she was confronted by her former guard, Corrie prayed “God be my forgiveness until I can forgive." This quotation whether accurate or not has provided a powerful prayer in many circumstances. Over the years I have prayed; "God be my forgiveness; God be my strength; God be my peace, God be my patience; God be my mercy; God be my joy…" The list is as long and varied as the situations, usually relational, but I can honestly say He has never let me down with that prayer.

It seems so simple yet is so powerful when we look to God for our needs instead of trying to do things on our own. You don't ever have to do it alone! Look up and find your God given strength. God is there, no matter how hard the struggle, and is willing and eager to provide the love we need to equip us in every circumstance. He's just waiting for you to ask Him and then move forward. Sadly, there were times I asked but then froze and failed to take the first step. Sometimes it was easier to believe the lies in my head that convinced me I was unworthy, incapable, incompetent or… the list goes on. I'm so grateful God is patient! Step out and see what He will do. He will equip you to do what you were tempted to believe was the impossible and in the process provide you with a level of love, peace and joy you could never have imagined possible!

Holy Father,

Thank You for the power You provide to transform my life and make me more like You. Please God, help me to have the courage and faith to reach up and give everything to You! In every circumstance, Lord, please give me the wisdom to invite, listen and allow You to change my heart and mind so that I can love others with compassion, humility, mercy and grace.

I ask this in Jesus Holy Name.

Amen.

God as Our Sentinel – He Is Watching Over Us

Kananaskis Country, Canadian Rockies, Alberta © Bob Crosby

In Kananaskis country majestic mountains soar against the brilliant blue Alberta sky while rivers and streams gurgle over ancient rock and vibrant alpine blossoms nod joyfully from their precarious perches. Squeezed in between rocks, they have just the right spot with just enough soil, just enough nutrients, just enough light and just enough wind to nurture them, grow them and carry their seed to ensure they will continue to thrive. The flowers in this photo are fireweed; the territorial flower of the Yukon. Every part of this plant is edible. Given the history of the Yukon and the trials of the early explorers in that harsh climate it seems fireweed is a highly appropriate choice to receive this honour. They may have warded off starvation for some and at the very least filled hungry tummies for others.

Aren't we all a bit like lowly yet magnificent weeds, profusely scattered around the world; clinging while we try to belong in our own little space, wanting to be nourished and nurtured, wanting to leave behind something life- giving and change -making for future generations, to help them meet their needs? You are not some cosmic accident; none of us are! We were created to fulfill God's plan "for such a time as this." Not only did He have a purpose in mind for each of us. God also promises "For I know the plans I have for you," declares the LORD, "plans to prosper you and not to harm you, plans to give you hope and a future." (Jeremiah 29:11)

It seems that the greater our need, the greater our joy in remembering God's watchful presence and provision; and the greater His glory! His provision for our basic needs during the tough times nourishes our body and nurtures our sense of wonder; but even greater than that is the sense of His loving presence; a kind of towering mountain in our lives. His incredible gifts of grace, mercy and love lead to a profound sense of awe and elation; and remembering such experiences can help us weather the winters of our lives. We can no more exist apart from God than the fireweed can. He alone provides just the right mixture to help us thrive and provide help to others. We only need to turn to Him with faith and trust; "Being confident of this, that He who began a good work in you will carry it on to completion until the day of Christ Jesus." (Philippians 1:6)

"I lift up my eyes to the mountains—
where does my help come from?
My help comes from the LORD,
the Maker of heaven and earth.

He will not let your foot slip—
he who watches over you will not slumber;
indeed, he who watches over Israel
will neither slumber nor sleep.

The LORD watches over you—
the LORD is your shade at your right hand;
the sun will not harm you by day, nor the moon by night.

The LORD will keep you from all harm—
he will watch over your life;
the LORD will watch over your coming and going
both now and forevermore. " (Psalm 121)

The Lord is watching over us. He sees our needs before we do and has a plan at the ready to come to our aid. Sometimes I wish I could see Him standing there in the flesh, as His disciples did. Then maybe, just maybe I'd be more confident and my faith would soar. After all they walked and talked with Jesus; witnessed His miracles and anticipated more. Still, they could also be just as thick as me, wondering how it could possibly be made right! Sometimes, even though Jesus might as well be standing right in front of me, my faith falters. Yet there are so many examples of why it shouldn't; I only need to remember!

"Lifting up his eyes, then, and seeing that a large crowd was coming toward him, Jesus said to Philip, 'Where are we to buy bread, so that these people may eat?' He said this to test him, for he himself knew what he would do. Philip answered him 'two hundred denarii worth of bread would not be enough for each of them to get a little.'

Andrew, Simon Peter's brother, said to him, 'There is a boy here who has five barley loaves and two fish, but what are they for so many?' Jesus said, 'Have the people sit down.' Now there was much grass in the place. So the men sat down, about five thousand in number.

Jesus then took the loaves, and when he had given thanks, he distributed them to those who were seated. So also the fish, as much as they wanted. And when they had eaten their fill, he told his disciples, 'Gather up the leftover fragments, that nothing may be lost.' So they gathered them up and filled twelve baskets with fragments from the five barley loaves left by those who had eaten." (Matthew 14: 17-20)

Who wouldn't love this story but is it applicable today? That was when Jesus walked on this planet and was physically present with the five thousand! When we pray, can we really trust that God hears us and will meet our most basic needs? When we're worried about job losses, finances, or where our next meal will come from, can we realistically expect God to come through? Is God really keeping watch over us during our darkest nights?

As a privileged middle class Canadian, I've never truly experienced hunger. There was always something in the fridge or cupboard to fill the gap. I have however hungered for God's intervention, especially when we experienced job losses and financial stress. We've had to sell our homes three times when we were forced to move to seek work. In the case of our first home it was at a great loss, essentially losing everything we'd saved for years to be able to purchase a home.

Thanks to a relatively fickle high tech industry, and companies closing or pulling out, my husband was let go a number of times. We had two children to support and I was mostly a stay at home mother with part time jobs to contribute to our finances, but never earning enough to support the family. There were times when my faith wavered and I'd find myself wandering the grocery aisles wondering how we were going to get through. I forgot to look up.

Prayer is an interesting thing. Sometimes we get an answer right away but sometimes we have to dangle over the cliff before God pulls us up; or maybe it's just that He was waiting for me to look to Him for provision instead of trying to creep towards the slippery slope of my own solutions. I was dangling through my own foolishness, forgetting to turn to him. Oh, I was praying but in retrospect am pretty sure the prayers were weak and more out of a sense of desperation than a faith that God would pull us through. I was still very young in my faith. "But when you ask, you must believe and not doubt, because the one who doubts is like a wave of the sea, blown and tossed by the wind." (James 1:6.)

I was being tossed alright, yet despite my weakness or maybe because of it God's "grace" was "sufficient" and His mercy astounding! Out of the blue I received a letter from the Ontario Teacher's Federation. Years earlier, when we were first married and I moved to the Ottawa area, I had done a bit of substitute teaching and taught summer school for a season, but since teaching jobs were very scarce, I hadn't had any significant work. You can imagine my joyful surprise when the letter informed me that they wanted to close out my Ontario Teachers' pension fund since I was no longer living or teaching in Ontario. I hadn't even considered that I might have money in a pension fund! I received a cheque for $2,000; enough to see us through until Bob was offered a new job soon after. It was an answer to prayer, a huge blessing at a time when we needed it most and further proof that God was watching over us. As spectacular and timely as this unknown money's arrival was, it seemed even more precious to realize that God was looking after our current circumstances.

On another occasion, Bob lost his job for the second time in less than two years, when foreign companies either shut down his department or pulled out from British Columbia altogether. Economically, B.C. was not the place to be in 1999 and so we decided that we would look for work in Calgary. We put our house on the market.

One lovely spring day our realtor called with the news. "Congratulations, it's sold!

Lord, I wanted the job to come first, then the house sale! I did my best to smile over the phone, thanked Dave and hung up the phone shaking my head. *Here we are Lord, jobless and now homeless with two young kids. What next*? Oddly though, I didn't feel any particular sense of panic or foreboding; I felt more like a third party calmly observing the situation. Back then this was uncharacteristic of me. Calm was not something I did very well at all!

This was one of those rare times when I felt I was being led to another location rather than moving forward by my will. I found myself drawn to the table in the next room where my Bible was sitting. I opened my Bible and started reading where I had left off. What is it Lord? *Keep reading* and so I did, a few more lines of scripture until my eyes fell on the wonderful words He had chosen for me at just that moment of my life: "Then they cried out to the Lord in their trouble, and he delivered them from their distress. He led them by a straight way to a city where they could settle. Let them give thanks to the Lord for his unfailing love and his wonderful deeds for mankind for he satisfies the thirsty and fills the hungry with good things." (Psalm 107: 6-9)

In that instant and for many weeks after, I experienced complete peace and overwhelming joy. God just kept blessing us. In one weekend trip to Calgary, Bob was interviewed, offered and accepted a job. Then with only a few hours left and after many hours of discouraging house hunting, we walked into an open house, made an offer and became the proud owners of our dream home. Blessing upon blessing! God even indulged me with little details. I thought I would miss the lush ferns that grow on the B.C. coast. No problem. The former owner had planted beautiful ferns along the window in the front garden. Since we were going to be putting our belongings in storage for about a month, I sadly gave away our aquarium. Imagine our delight when my daughter discovered baby fish had hatched and were swimming around in the pond in our backyard. Year after year we upsized aquariums for the winter and watched them thrive and grow. They were further proof of God's abundant gifts to us beyond what we could have imagined.

We had twelve great years in Calgary but they weren't without challenges and periods of unemployment. Bob's company switched hands; he was unemployed again for a spell. Then the company that hired him decided to leave town. Though they wanted to transfer him back east, his heart was in the west. Job searches in Calgary yielded nothing.

He did finally secure a job but it meant another move back to the coast. Bob was thrilled. I wasn't, mainly because of the people we left behind; especially our children and now grandchildren too! Still, I'm trying. I know God is in this. He has a lesson for me and blessings yet to bestow. Remembering past experiences with God encourages me for the future.

It doesn't mean we always get what we ask for; only God knows what's best for us and He often allows us to experience pain, loss and even the death of loved ones. When Bob was out of work the last time in Calgary I told him I was willing to have him look on Vancouver Island stating "if you ever want me to leave Calgary you better do it while my parents are still alive." My parents were quite elderly by then and living in Nanaimo B.C. I was worried that a move would mean leaving our adult children behind but by then they were quite independent and I felt that my parents probably needed us more. I delighted in the thought of Mom's joy at being able to get out and go places with me and Dad's thrill at having more family nearby.

I still regret that statement of ultimatum I made to my husband and sometimes wonder if it was such arrogance and egotistical bull headedness that contributed to our sorrow. Who was I to demand the future and make plans accordingly! Could Bob have found another job in Calgary if I hadn't so emotionally blurted out the other option? We'd had that conversation before. I loved Calgary and told him I never wanted to leave unless it was for my parents. I know God has forgiven me but it still grates on my conscience at times.

Sadly, two weeks before we moved back to Vancouver Island my mother unexpectedly suffered a stroke and passed away. It was almost more than I could bear that September, leaving everything behind and moving to a new life with its gaping hole of grief. It was as if a mudslide of misery had come hurtling down over my life and wiped out everyone and everything I held dear. Besides giving up my family, extended family; church "family" and dear friends in Calgary, I'd had to leave my teaching career; the wonderful immigrants in my class and lovely colleagues who all made my job such a joy! I was quite overwhelmed with sorrow. I had made many moves in my lifetime, both as a child and later as a wife. However, this was the only move I ever made that in the end held not one element of excitement and happiness.

Still, I trust God knew what He was doing. In Isaiah 57:1 we are told, "The righteous perish, and no one ponders it in his heart; devout men are taken away, and no one understands that the righteous are taken away to be spared from evil. Those who walk uprightly enter into peace; they find rest as they lie in death." God had no doubt seen how Mom had stoically suffered through pain for many years, "taking up her cross" without complaint; and as my Dad sometimes remarked "soldiering on." My mom had been one of 12 siblings and like a number of them signed up to serve her country. She joined the Canadian Women's Army Corp during World War II and left the military shortly after the war ended and she married our Dad. Mom served as devotedly in her later life; always with a strong sense of what was right and always with kindness.

Now, she was in God's arms. She was finally free of pain and physical effort and at the very least, I was glad I was closer by so Dad didn't have to feel quite so alone. It was good to be able to offer him some hands on help together with my siblings after he sold the house.

God had watched over Mom for decades, blessed her with a quiet wisdom, love for her family along with many other neighbours and friends, and an incredible grace towards others. Though she was quiet and unassuming if she believed in something she showed no fear or backing down. I still remember the time as a young student walking to school I got stuck in a large mud puddle by a construction site. I couldn't get my boots free from the gooey mess and didn't want to step out of them. Those were the days when parents felt safe letting their kids walk a mile or so to school in the company of others. I was either in kindergarten or grade one at the time. My friends had all given up not wanting to be late and gone on without me.

Even then God was watching over me. A nearby neighbour heard me crying and saw my predicament. She helped rescue me and got me home to my mother. That very afternoon Mom, with me in tow, took to knocking on doors getting a petition signed. She phoned the mayor and informed him that none of the children in our neighbourhood would be attending school the next day unless a bus was there to pick us up.

I was too young to know at the time but many of the neighbours had been concerned about the construction site along our route especially with the rainy season. They were afraid that a child might fall into one of many holes dug for future basements and this had been part of the petition's argument for a bus. My Mom the social activist; thank God that I got stuck in the mud and He equipped her to do His work before a real tragedy occurred. Maybe it never would have but I still know God was in it all and I believe that He never wastes circumstances. He works things we may never know into good for people we may never know. He made Mom who she was, dare I say it, maybe even "for such a time as this." (Esther 4:14) I know it's a stretch and forgive this daughter's heart but when Mom had her mind set on the greater good there was no turning her away, just a little like Queen Esther. Not much later the call came in that there would be a bus in the morning. None of us ever had to walk through that construction site again.

As painful as Mom's passing was and as crushed as I was when my mother was taken away and I was robbed of all my foolishly dreamed plans of taking her places and doing things together, I had to concede that nothing I could share with her could ever be as glorious as where she now resides! Since her girls were far away, and Mom didn't drive, whenever we girls would come for a visit, she'd love having us take her to the mall and wander the stores, maybe go for a cup of coffee or in the summer some sweet ice cream. Later on my dad was on a restricted diet and Mom would never eat ice cream when he was with her because she didn't want him to feel he was missing out. She just had that kind of a sacrificial caring heart. We didn't have to buy anything either; she just enjoyed the looking and being together with her girls as much as anything. Seriously though, did I really think wandering a mall together, or coffee or even ice cream would be fantastic for her, especially in light of her current place of residence!

Since then we had to say goodbye to our dad too, another soldier who toiled long and hard for his family and so many others. Now, though I miss them both completely, I have the joy of knowing that they are together again, in the perfect love, peace and joy of our Saviour and being spared from "the "evil" in this world. Both would often recoil in horror with the news of yet another cruelty happening around the world. They have been spared a lot of evil!

Over the years I've prayed for many to be healed and live. Some have and some haven't. Still I trust that God has been keeping watch and knew exactly what He was doing. He has His own infinitely wise reasons that I can't possibly fathom and graciously loves each of us enough to take us home to Him exactly when we should go. When tragedies strike, it is hard to understand why God allowed them to take place but somewhere deep inside I've reconciled such news and found comfort with the thought that perhaps by taking those people when He did, He was sparing them and possibly even others from something far worse.

Holy Father,

Thank You for watching over us with your deep love and affection, and providing for all our needs in all our circumstances! Please help us to remember with grateful hearts all the times You've protected, and nurtured us. When we're struggling and feeling choked and alone Lord, please guide our thoughts and prayers back to You!

In Jesus Name.

Amen.

When It Seems Impossible – God is Our Miracle Maker

Brilliant Light and Gathering Storm, Highway to Lethbridge, Alberta

© Bob Crosby

Sitting in our tiny little vehicle as it was rocking with the ferocious southern Alberta wind, while my husband was out in the middle of the highway trying to get the perfect picture I was quite fearful; fearful a vehicle would come out of nowhere and strike Bob or our vehicle would be tossed over into the ditch with me inside it. Perhaps only photographers and their spouses will get what lengths a shutterbug will go to for that perfect shot. I've had lots of tense moments throughout my married life encouraging Bob to "be careful" and "please hurry!" This was always a wasted sentence. I've decided Photographers never "hurry."

Love and life can be a bit like that; the brilliance in a storm, rugged beauty and fearsome raging, the fear of what lies ahead and the urge to run in the opposite direction yet the overpowering desire to stay long enough to capture that perfect shot. After all we only have one life to live so we'd better make it a good one!

I have to be honest. I don't like waiting for God. It would be so much easier, and often neater and tidier if He could just step in early. However, I am convinced that it is those times when we feel completely out of control and needing His provision in our lives, that we gain the added blessing of hugging Him tight, remembering His provision in the past, building our relationship with Him in the present and soaking in His deep love for His children. Out of our greater needs, comes our greater gladness. Would our hearts soar so high in His Presence if we had never experienced the trials and the hard times of feeling alone; times of praying and waiting that felt like divine silence?

"The Spirit of the Sovereign LORD is on me, because the LORD has anointed me to proclaim good news to the poor. He has sent me to bind up the broken-hearted, to proclaim freedom for the captives and release from darkness for the prisoners, to proclaim the year of the LORD's favor and the day of vengeance of our God, to comfort all who mourn, and provide for those who grieve in Zion- to bestow on them a crown of beauty instead of ashes, the oil of joy instead of mourning, and a garment of praise instead of a spirit of despair. They will be called oaks of righteousness, a planting of the LORD for the display of his splendor." (Isaiah 61:1-3)

Truthfully, I'd rather not have the hardships and trials but I wouldn't trade them if it meant missing out on Him! God brings us out of the ashes into beauty in His time. Lifting us from our mourning, God bathes us in His "oil of joy." He replaces our despair with exuberant praise so that all will see His glory. God's very presence in our lives is miraculous enough, yet He willingly takes our pain, sorrow, sin and trials, turns them into foundations for His praise and in the process blesses us completely!

"It was about this time that King Herod arrested some who belonged to the church, intending to persecute them. He had James, the brother of John, put to death with the sword. When he saw that this met with approval among the Jews, he proceeded to seize Peter also. This happened during the Festival of Unleavened Bread. After arresting him, he put him in prison, handing him over to be guarded by four squads of four soldiers each. Herod intended to bring him out for public trial after the Passover.

So Peter was kept in prison, but the church was earnestly praying to God for him.

The night before Herod was to bring him to trial, Peter was sleeping between two soldiers, bound with two chains, and sentries stood guard at the entrance. Suddenly an angel of the Lord appeared and a light shone in the cell. He struck Peter on the side and woke him up. "Quick, get up!" he said, and the chains fell off Peter's wrists.

Then the angel said to him, "Put on your clothes and sandals." And Peter did so. "Wrap your cloak around you and follow me," the angel told him. Peter followed him out of the prison, but he had no idea that what the angel was doing was really happening; he thought he was seeing a vision. They passed the first and second guards and came to the Iron Gate leading to the city. It opened for them by itself, and they went through it. When they had walked the length of one street, suddenly the angel left him.

Then Peter came to himself and said, "Now I know without a doubt that the Lord has sent his angel and rescued me from Herod's clutches and from everything the Jewish people were hoping would happen." (Acts 12:1-11)

Are you having or have you had those moments in your life when you just really didn't know what you were going to do? One worship song, God will Make a Way by Don Moen seemed like my theme song over multiple years and a variety of circumstances. I sang the words, "God will make a way when there seems to be no way" so often; always believing in God's power but wondering would He, and if so, when would He rescue me?

Sometimes our waiting can seem interminable but then our circumstances change in a heartbeat. Though it is from a different kind of prison, like Peter, we are released from whatever has us in chains, and we feel like we must be dreaming. Sometimes it's a little thing, sometimes it's huge, but always it carries the unmistakable imprint of our Father God, looking after his lost sheep and providing for us in our time of need in some remarkable way. He puts people in our lives that seem like they must be angels. "Are not all angels ministering spirits sent to serve those who will inherit salvation?" (Hebrews 1: 14) I'd love to see one with fluffy white wings, carrying a trumpet but the reality is that most of the angels I've been able to see have been even better than that. They have been people I knew and loved and even a few strangers.

I remember one time arriving at an airport late at night. I was on my way to visit my then elderly parents. Somehow our communication wires had gotten crossed and I was standing alone outside of the airport without a taxi in sight. Before I'd even had time to pray about it, a lady who had been with me on my flight approached; she realized something was amiss and asked if she and her daughter could help. Her daughter kindly drove out of her way to get me to my parent's home.

God has so often put the people I need at that very moment in my path. On another occasion I was on a train heading to Munich to meet up with my husband. Other than a few polite phrases in German I had nothing to communicate with. I had expected one train stop for "Munchen" but as we approached suddenly realized there were at least two or three. I was starting to panic as I had no idea which stop I should disembark at and the steward on my car had made it clear he didn't speak English. Again, at just the right time and only moments before pulling into the first station God placed a gentleman in my path who managed to use just enough English to make it clear that I should take the next stop. I don't remember how or why he knew I needed direction. I'm sure that was another of God's gifts to me; another one of His "ministering spirits" to help me along when I was lost and needing direction.

It's such a thrill to see God's response to meet our needs! Neither of those situations would have been earth shattering but it did my heart good to see God's love at work, showing me I never needed to be alone; He had me covered and still does. Now during times of stress I try to relax and remember that He will come through in time and even if I would like that to happen sooner than later I can still fully trust He's on my side. Sometimes the little whimsical miracles seem even more meaningful than the big ones. God's got better things to do with His energy but He cares enough to reach down to each one of us with His precious gift of undeserved favour!

My husband and I experienced another little miracle this past year. Let me back up; seven years prior, while biking to work, Bob's wedding band must have slipped off his finger. He couldn't find it anywhere, though he retraced the bike route. He was working on the University of Victoria campus at the time and regularly checked in with campus security but it was not to be found. Fast forward to 2018 and one day when I was just talking to my Heavenly Father. Sometime during my prayer time the thought of the lost ring popped up. "God," said I, "I know this is such a little thing compared to everything else you're looking after, but I sure would love it if we found Bob's ring. I understand if you have more important things to do but if it's okay, would you please bring it back to us?"

Just about a month later our daughter who lived in Calgary contacted us to say that my sister had shared a Facebook post and picture of a wedding ring. Stephanie recognized it immediately as her Dad's. My sister had no idea it was Bob's but our daughter knew. The kind man who found it said he thought he'd just try one more time on social media since he knew it had to be important to someone. He'd been hanging onto it for us for seven years! That was quite the answer to prayer and felt like such a love letter from my Heavenly Father! Bob now has it firmly back on his finger and I delight every time I think of how God blessed us by answering my little prayer.

Holy Father,

Thank You for the miraculous blessing of your love and perfectly timed intervention when all else seems hopelessly lost. By your Holy Spirit power help us to never lose sight of your goodness and mercy. Help us to always remember and trust that You are there for us in the good times and the hard times. Forgive me for the times I've forgotten and faltered, turning to self instead of to You. Let us never stop seeking your will and glorifying You!

In Jesus Holy Name.

Amen.

God is Our First Responder - In Every Situation Call on Him

Sackville Waterfowl Park, Sackville, New Brunswick © Bob Crosby

This beautiful boardwalk winds its way through the Sackville Waterfowl Park, an oases to over 150 species of birds and 200 species of plants. Walking along the boardwalk one early evening I was awed by the vision; light dancing on the water and between the trees; and the sounds of bird calls filling this reclaimed marshland with a summer symphony. At one time farmers toiled to fill in the marsh and work its fertile soil for agriculture. It fed and housed families many years before a small group of people envisioned its current use. A number of residents took a proposed idea to support local businesses by revitalizing the downtown and worked to make it happen. Their proposal was to reclaim the marshland and create a place for locals, tourists and wildlife alike.

There is often resistance to any kind of change, never mind one with such an impact on the landscape as we've come to know it. One can only begin to imagine the perseverance it took to stand firm against the detractors in their community and promote their plan to once again flood the wetland. The idea was born in 1984. It took two more years to gain an "agreement in principle." They needed to gain approval and funding before it would move forward. It would be another two years of effort, not knowing if it would ever happen but it did and in 1988 the marshland was reborn. In the midst of our challenges we rarely know the final outcome. It would be so easy to sit back and declare it over with; a done non-deal. It would take a miracle and that won't ever happen!

Except, it can and it does; and while we may not know the outcome, if we turn our backs on our God given passions and opt out of the effort required we may miss blessings far beyond those for ourselves! How many generations will walk and delight in the miracle of the Sackville Marsh? How many children will explore and learn thanks to a group of people who wouldn't give up?

Who are we to back up if God is trying to move us forward? The worst that can happen is that our plan fails to come to fruition but if we're praying about it and God is in the middle even that option could lead to blessings. We don't know if the effort we put in helped to encourage others in completely different endeavours that could have lasting benefits, helped to cement relationships or provided preparation for something else God wants to call us to do. It may have been part of the process toward a more important endeavour. We just need to be available and persevere! The only way to do that well is by staying connected to God in prayer, through His word and with fellow believers. Nourishing our souls in nature doesn't hurt either. It can bring further peace and strength for whatever challenge is weighing us down and provide moments of delight surrounded by God's creative beauty.

"If you abide in Me, and My words abide in you, ask whatever you wish, and it will be done for you." (John 15:7)

When we stop to look, we can often see how God answers prayers and meets us miraculously in both the big and small things. In the process, He helps others we love and sometimes strangers too. One of my favourite blessings started with deep sadness. I was preparing to start my afternoon English class when one of my students approached me. "Teacher, please can I leave class," Ana began to cry and through her tears explained that she had just received news that both of her parents were very ill in hospital in Colombia. Without thinking I asked Ana if I could pray with her. We stepped inside the cloak room and prayed. I knew Ana couldn't afford to go to

Colombia, but found myself praying that God would make a way for her to be able to go home and be with her parents. That was on Thursday afternoon.

That Sunday, I woke up with an idea. My husband was performing a Latin American themed concert with the Calgary Concert Band. Was this a coincidence? I don't think so. Still I wondered if I was following God or trying to do something on my own. After much prayer I still felt it was the right thing and thought I'd rather do what I felt compelled to do than miss the chance to please God and help Ana. Besides I figured if I got it wrong, God would know that it was born out of a desire to serve Him and still forgive me. I went to my computer and printed off one simple sign in large bold letters, "For Ana." I took a basket and my Chinook Learning name badge as some weak sort of proof that I was who I said I was and left for church.

After church my kids and I headed to the concert hall. I kept praying along the way and asked God to open the door wide if I was supposed to do this and make it clear if I was mistaken. In the corridor at the Rozsa Centre theatre, the first person I saw was the band's conductor walking towards me. I explained Ana's situation and asked if I would be able to take up a collection for her. There was not the slightest hesitation on his part. "Absolutely, I'll announce it just before intermission." It seemed like an open door to me!

Finally the big moment arrived. The conductor made the announcement and I headed into the lobby with my sign and basket. A few people came and made donations. The bell rang. Intermission was over. I looked in my basket with dismay. I had about sixty five dollars of the total $3,000 we needed so that Ana could return to Columbia with her young son. Oh no, what have I done! Until that moment it never occurred to me that if I didn't raise enough money it would be impossible to give it back to the anonymous donors. I wasn't a charitable organization, I couldn't even offer a tax slip, yet these good people were willing to donate on my word alone. Now what?

I no sooner had those discouraging thoughts cross my mind when God answered. It was crystal clear and almost seemed audible though it was more likely powerfully placed in my mind. "*Don't forget the loaves and the fishes*!" Peace flooded my soul. "*You're right Lord; you're bigger than our wallets and our plans. You alone will make this happen.*"

With the exception of His free gift of salvation, I don't know if God ever gives us what we ask for without some effort on our part. Of course, I still had work to do to help Ana. I wrote letters and made phone calls, talked to my church, colleagues and friends. People I didn't know made donations from across Calgary. Students in my class wanted to help their classmate and gave too, often out of their own financial challenges. When I tried to contact a Latino church I got the church where they used to meet. Harvest Hills provided me with the new phone number and a generous donation of their own. About one week in, almost half the fare was sitting in a bank account. I told more friends and one suggested I try CJAY 92, a local radio station that was giving away money to help people in need. I contacted the lady overseeing their Secret Wish program. She asked me to submit a letter explaining why I thought Ana and her family should be the recipients. I got started right away, sent it off as soon as I could get it written and explained that there was a time issue with her parents being so ill. God blessed this effort. The radio station decided to help and I was to arrange to get their representative into Ana's apartment building early in the morning so they could surprise her on air at 7:40 a.m. I'm afraid I told a bit of a lie to accomplish this. I told Ana and her husband I wanted to deliver the money we had collected (true), and I had to bring it early because we were going camping (I was going camping but I had no intention of leaving that early.) I also apologized that it wasn't enough when I knew more was coming!

I sat in the living room chatting with them and waiting for the phone call from the radio station. It came. Her husband answered and was a little confused at first but when he followed their instructions and opened the door, there was Kelly with her gifts for the family. The radio station realized they needed the money for the trip more than other things so gave a larger amount than usual, but she also brought a huge bag of toys for Ana's son, a gift card for Wal-Mart and if my memory serves me right, also one for a local grocery store. Once again God demonstrated that He "is able to do immeasurably more than all we ask or imagine, according to his power that is at work within us" (Ephesians 3:20.) In the end they had a little more than what was needed for the tickets. They were overwhelmed and the joy was palpable.

There's more though! God had to intervene miraculously again before Ana could go. Ana discovered that her Colombian passport had expired. The only way for her to get it renewed was to go to the consulate in Vancouver. There was enough money to fly home but certainly not enough for a trip to Vancouver too. Then good news arrived. It just so happened that the very next week, a representative from the Colombian Consulate was making a special trip to Calgary to help renew passports. That day, Ana walked into the office and out again holding her renewed passport which was paid for by the rest of the donations. We had no idea, but God knew exactly how much she needed and it was there in the bank account.

Ana and her son went off to Colombia. They were able to spend time loving & comforting her parents, sister and extended family. It was God's huge gift to Ana and her family. The interesting thing is that it was a huge blessing for me also. I'm so grateful I listened and stepped out when God called. I'm sure it was His plan all along and He would have got Ana home but what a privilege and honour to get to be a part of it all!

I've had other experiences when God answered my prayers though not quite so quickly. Twice it was for protection and help for my children who were going through very difficult experiences. After many hours/ years of crying out to God along with my faithful sisters and brothers in Christ who prayed for us too, everything we prayed for them came to pass. They both came safely through very dark periods in their lives but there's more on this later. Life's challenges persist and I still keep praying for them. I don't know how children survive and parents manage without God's hand on our kids. We need to pray daily for them and our grandkids too!

I once spent many months praying through a difficult work situation. I was very new on the job and had taken over from a talented lady who had worked there a number of years. She and my boss had become close friends. It must have been very challenging for my boss to have to put up with this newcomer who didn't always understand what was expected. I was feeling discouraged, working very hard but never seemingly able to understand completely or live up to what was wanted from me. As a recovering people pleaser – well, I'm working on it - this was really taking its toll! Throughout my working career, I had rarely received anything less than a glowing report. Of course there were always ways to improve and though I always preferred hearing the positive feedback most, I was fine with constructive criticism and generally agreed with the assessments. In this case though, I had never felt so isolated and undervalued. At one point my husband wanted me to quit, but I didn't want to go that way. I prayed and prayed for this boss, even finding myself praying one morning that we might become friends. I almost laughed out loud with that one; it was definitely asking for the impossible! Or was it? Within a few months we were on friendly terms and the displeasure had dissolved. When I left due to a move, I was blessed with a beautiful card, generous gift and message of appreciation. That could only have been God's doing. The improved communication and turnaround in our relationship certainly was more than I could have imagined a few months earlier.

It seems to me such an overwhelmingly extravagant gift God gave us when He allows us to speak with Him and pour out our hearts in both the wonderful and the dark and difficult times. I really would encourage all of us to persevere in prayer and remember His promise in Philippians "Rejoice in the Lord always; I will say it again: rejoice! Let your gentleness be evident to all. The Lord is near. Be anxious about nothing but in every situation, by prayer and petition, with thanksgiving, present your requests to God. And the peace of God, which transcends all understanding, will guard your hearts and your minds in Christ Jesus." (Philippians 4: 4-9) As difficult as rejoicing can be in the face of difficult realities and life experiences, somehow when we can lean into God's peace and really grasp that He will keep us as close as His beloved Son and "guard our hearts and minds in Christ Jesus," those experiences become so much more bearable.

Holy Father,

Thank You for the blessing and privilege of prayer, and your words of counsel throughout the Bible teaching us to pray and not give up.
Lord, through your Holy Spirit power, please help us to diligently pray, unceasingly and with great faith, for the people You bring to us for prayer. Where words fail; let your Holy Spirit continue to intercede for us, according to your promise in Romans 8:26 and to your good and perfect will. Please keep us all close and trusting in You and in the name of your son Jesus Christ! We can do nothing without You but are grateful that with You, everything is possible.
In Jesus Name we pray.
Amen.

When God Answers In a Heartbeat or When He Doesn't

Niagara Falls, Goldstream Provincial Park, Vancouver Island, British Columbia © Bob Crosby

My favourite time to be at Goldstream Park, near Victoria, British Columbia is in the fall. Spawning salmon remind me of God's creative work and remarkable plans for nature. Seeing those dying salmon, filled with supernatural strength as they work hard to fulfill their purpose and ensure survival is awe inspiring. Even though life can be messy and smelly sometimes, God is there through it all. The salmon won't live to see their offspring hatch but their work is an act of faith and ultimately it goes rewarded as shiny little fry continue the cycle.

Though it's messy, beauty prevails here too with brightly coloured leaves forming a soft carpet underfoot that glistens with moisture on the smooth rocks of the river bed. I have seen that river filled with raging torrents of water in the spring, but most often in the summer and fall a section under the highway is empty and the tourists who gather there have no trouble walking over it to get to Niagara Falls. It's true; that is what it is called, but is not to be confused with Niagara Falls in Ontario and New York State! Heading out to see Goldstream's Niagara Falls is an easy trail for me until I reach the culvert that runs under the Island Highway. Coming out of the daylight into that darkened tunnel, my footsteps slow and my body tenses. Even though I remind myself it's perfectly safe, my head is trying to tell me otherwise. I keep going, carefully picking my steps in the gloomy shadows. It's a bit like stepping out in obedience to my Heavenly Father; a little disconcerting, sometimes frightening, but always worth it. There may be voices of discouragement, for me there often are; and I can't see where I'm going. Still I know it will lead me to something beautiful; a lovely waterfall cascading into the rocks. God's living water refreshing my soul!

"The Lord had said to Abram, "Leave your country, your people and your father's household and go to the land I will show you; I will make you into a great nation and I will bless you' I will make your name great, and you will be a blessing. I will bless those who bless you, and whoever curses you I will curse; and all peoples on earth will be blessed through you."
So Abram left, as the Lord had told him; and Lot went with him. Abram was seventy-five years old when he set out from Haran." (Genesis 12: 1- 4)

Have you been there? Felt the need to move forward but not sure which direction to take? I wonder if Abram/Abraham and Sarai/ Sarah felt the same way. *Seriously God, seventy-five and now you want me to pack up and leave the life we've built here?*

Poor Sarai, how hard would it have been for her to say goodbye to people she loved and head out for the great unknown? I've had a little, no, quite a lot of experience with that, but with modern technology that helps me keep in touch and transportation that ensures I can get to see people again, my life changes haven't been nearly as difficult, albeit I'm sure they were just as heart wrenching. I hate goodbyes!

Sometimes it's easier to praise God than others. I just had to leave my family and friends behind after spending three glorious months in our old home city of Calgary, babysitting the sweetest little girl alive; our first grandchild! Calgary is my heart home because of the people I love who live there and there is never a departure that doesn't leave me sad. Yet today the sorrow is miraculously mixed with joy. I can't explain it; it just is. This is God's gift to me.

It's January; a month that is often rainy and grey. Yet, sunshine is streaming through my window. Crows are noisily gathering to celebrate the morning and I was awakened by the unmistakable call of a gull soaring over the Pacific blue. My heart is full which is the main reason or the only reason I'm sitting at my computer now. I'm not even sure what I'm going to write about today, just that the song of praise filled my mind and somehow I want to give it wings.

Today's blessings may be connected to a couple of things; First, a desire to draw nearer to God and second a desire to walk in obedience.

I need to let you know, that while I passionately long to be closer to God, I struggle with that. I am so easily distracted by life! I'm often reminded of Paul's cry; "I do not understand what I do. For what I want to do I do not do, but what I hate I do." (Romans 7:15)

I can relate to Paul's sentiment in so many ways. Paralysis too often steps in when it comes to starting a task. "I do not do what I want to do!" That's been an ongoing challenge with my writing for probably at least three years. I have been keenly aware that God gave me such a passion for writing that I should be doing it, but instead I listened to the voice of discouragement and lies; *you a writer? Do you really think God wants you to write? What makes you think you could do that? Besides, you don't have time!*

I was quite thrilled one morning a few days ago to hear those whispers, recognize where they were coming from and firmly rebuke them. *NO- Only God would wake me with a directive to write a travel devotional so this is exactly what I should be doing! I couldn't possibly do that on my strength, but God can and He's going to equip me to be able to write it. So you can just go away!*

Do you experience such discouraging whispers and lies; or maybe conflict, gossip or ugly thoughts? I've experienced it all but God brought my dear friend Adrianne into my life and she taught me one thing I could do. I love how she handles such situations. Adrianne simply says "Jesus, Satan's knocking. Will you please get that?" I've adopted this practice frequently and am happy to say He always does! Not that the circumstances always change, but God takes care of it so I can enjoy His "peace that surpasses all understanding." (Philippians 4:7)

I also too often let busyness get between me and what God really wanted me to do; *I need to look after the people in my life, volunteer at my church and in my community, look after my housework – after all, what would people think of me if they knew....* Knew what; that my house gets messy and dirty? (Join the club ;) That my meals aren't gourmet? (Who cares? They're usually nutritious- and at the very least they fill the gap ;) That I get tired and need to rest? (Even Jesus had to rest!)

These are just a few examples. I'm sure there are more! Have you been there? None of those measuring sticks are inherently wrong. Helping others and being good stewards of the gifts God has given us, such as our families and homes, are worthy pursuits. They can be so very good but like every coin, they can be flipped. I taught Sunday school. I loved it and I loved the kids but the last few years after I moved to Victoria, I realized I hadn't prayed about what God wanted me to do for my church. I just knew there was a need and good old small "s" saviour Debbie just had to step in and offer to teach. Really? I cringe now, *God forgive my arrogance*!

Still God is gracious; He let me teach, and he equipped me, but my heart wasn't in it to the same extent it used to be. Sometimes I found myself resentful about the preparation time and then I felt guilty; as much because of my resentful heart as for the fact that I could tell that I was doing it for the wrong reasons. Even though I loved the kids and fully enjoyed my time with them, I didn't feel like I was fully serving God in the way He wants to be served - with a joyful heart! The times that I have been working with and for God I was energized, excited and full of joy but this was not happening.

For at least two or more years, I never felt completely certain about what God wanted from me and just kept muddling along saying yes to things that needed doing. Then at a Children's Christmas presentation while visiting my old home church Northwest Community church in Calgary, we were challenged – "What gift will you bring the King this year?" I was so moved by that simple question and went home fervently praying about what I could give. I did have a little idea based on a workshop I had recently attended for a Calgary charity, Gems for Gems, that helps women in shelters. I thought perhaps I could get a chapter started here in Nanaimo; I still might but I need to pray about it to make sure it really is God moving me to serve in this direction and not just my head running ahead of Him again.

The funny thing with this Christmas challenge was that despite my passion for writing, it never even crossed my mind. I had been absolutely stalled with my writing; prayed lots, attempted it a few times but never really felt it from my heart. I still enjoyed any time that I spent writing but there wasn't the level of joy I was used to or more importantly the draw to keep coming back. I could easily walk away for months distracted by all the other demands on my time.

I had been skirting around writing ideas for a number of years since about 2013 when I was ill with Lyme disease. At that time, I thought I was meant to write stories for my Victoria congregation; interviewing people who wanted to share a story about when God met them to encourage our church body. I wrote a grand total of three stories. The ladies who shared and a few others said they loved them but that was it. It just all fizzled out. It seemed strange because at that time I absolutely believed that was what God had wanted from me. I was too sick to take on any physical roles but I could sit, interview and write about the times God intervened for His children. Did I get it all wrong and only think that was how He wanted me to serve?

I started to question my prayer life and whether God had given up on me. Was He punishing me for my sinful lack of gratitude? As you know our move from Calgary to Victoria had been very difficult for me due to grieving for my mother and everyone I'd left behind. I loved Calgary and more importantly my family and friends there. It was a struggle to be joyful and grateful; and trust that God was in it all. I couldn't blame Him if He did want to punish me but in reality, God doesn't work that way. He is the ultimate loving parent and we are His children! We wouldn't treat our own children that way so why would we even imagine that God would. "Which of you fathers, if your son asks for a fish, will give him a snake instead? Or if he asks for an egg, will give him a scorpion? If you then, though you are evil, know how to give good gifts to your children, how much more will your Father in heaven give the Holy Spirit to those who ask Him!" (Luke 11: 11-14)

Still at that time, I wondered about what sins I was committing; trying to do things on my own without recognizing God's sovereign control; procrastinating on things He wanted but going ahead on my own; my wavering faith and lack of trust in Him (?) How often had I just stepped in to a perceived need without really praying about it? Was I praying enough or hard enough? Was

I praying too little too late or especially with my writing, was I spinning my wheels maybe just because I didn't have enough courage to move forward?

On the other hand maybe God just had to grow me more to get me to the place where I was ready for more; the old "If you are faithful in little things, you will be faithful in large ones. But if you are dishonest in little things, you won't be honest with greater responsibilities."(Luke 16:10) Maybe I had to exercise my faithfulness and put it into action a little longer before He would move me ahead. You may have noticed; unfortunately I'm really good at second guessing which often makes my Christian walk a big challenge, but I'm so grateful God is faithful, merciful and gracious! He never really does give up on any of us!

Bob and I had also spent a number of years, off and on, wondering about writing a book that would include his photography as illustrations. I love his work, but I could never quite get my head around what kind of book I could write to go with it; a children's story; a travel book? Neither felt quite right.

Then, a couple of days before Christmas I woke up with a crystal clear answer to my prayerful question "What can I bring the King this year?" The answer may not have been audible but was so very real that I talked to my husband Bob about using his photos that very morning. My husband is not yet a believer but God still blesses me through him and I have infinite hope that God will answer my prayers for all my unbelieving family and friends. God knew what Saul needed to turn to Him and He knows what my loved ones need too. I often pray that I will see it in my lifetime but I trust either way that God will redeem each one of them!

That particular morning asking Bob about using his photos, Bob was all in. Bob's reaction is often a measuring stick I use to know if God really wants me to do something. When Bob is agreeable and there is peace between us I believe God is at work. I sat down immediately, started working to obey God's directive and started writing this travel devotional. I could barely keep up with the thoughts and words. They were flowing so quickly.

When I finished a few hours later I had a draft for my first chapter and was so overcome with joy and the excitement of being in God's presence that I told Bob "You have no idea how good this felt! I am so overwhelmed with joy; I need to write – regularly!"

Bob has been patiently supportive; I have been leaving the distractions and coming quite regularly to my desk to write. It has been a beautiful time! As I write this, it's really just a very rough draft yet but it is filling me up. There are times when I start and I don't know what I'm going to write but God brings me memories, and worship songs to sing, and it is, if nothing else, a wonderful time of devotion.

It encourages me to think that my walk with God is ongoing and He looks after the problems in His time. Should I strive to be closer to Him and behave more like Him? Absolutely! Do I have to do it on my own strength? Absolutely NOT!

There are only two things I need to do to ensure that I can get closer to Him. First I pray. I pray for the Holy Spirit to take my thoughts, words and actions captive. I pray on the armour of God and I ask that He alone will direct my path and fill me with a very real sense of His presence. "Therefore put on the full armor of God, so that when the day of evil comes, you may be able to stand your ground, and after you have done everything, to stand." (Ephesians 6: 13) For those unaccustomed to praying on God's armour this is how I pray: Holy Father, Please place your armour of protection over me; your sandals of the peace of the gospel on my feet to guide my steps; your belt of truth around my waist to keep me honest and true; your breastplate of righteousness over my heart to guard my emotions and let your fruits of the spirit; your Love, Joy, Peace, Patience, Kindness, Goodness, Gentleness, Righteousness and Self-Control be evident and offered to Bob, my family, my friends and all those I meet with today. Please place your helmet of Salvation over my head. Cover what I think, see, hear and say and let it all be to your glory. Place your shield of faith in my left hand. Let me cling firmly to it. When Satan's fiery arrows come at me let them clink and fall and fizzle out before they can harm me or anyone else. "Let me stand and when I have done everything, still stand (Ephesians 6:13);" and place your sword of the Spirit, Your Holy Word in my right hand. "Let Your Word be a lamp unto my feet and a light unto my path."(Psalm 119:105) In Jesus Name I Pray. Amen.

I was taught this practice of praying on God's armour decades ago and when I first started, it was sporadic. Somewhere along the way I started to recognize, on days when things just all seemed to be out of whack and I was feeling out of sorts, that I'd forgotten to pray on the armour of God. I'd pray it on and things always improved. Now it is unusual for me to get out of bed in the morning without first praying on His armour. It has made a huge difference in my life.

After I pray on God's armour, I go to His word. I can't read the Bible without feeling closer to God. Sometimes I struggle with that too. I'm so easily distracted but I keep reading and re-reading – sometimes only a very short passage over and over, until I can settle in, understand a little better and know I am with Him.

Another huge help has been to remain in fellowship and prayer with other believers. I am incredibly blessed to have many godly, faithful believers in my life. We lift each other up in prayer, listen to each other, celebrate the joys, share each other's tears and when God guides us, may offer up words of wisdom and/or discernment to help each other. Hearing each other's faith stories helps us to remember that God's promises are real and encourages us in the trials. My beautiful sisters and brothers in Christ have encouraged and mentored me along the way. God has often used them to deliver His wisdom and direction and I am grateful!

God promises "Ask and it will be given to you, Seek and you will find, Knock and the door will be opened to you." (Matthew 7:7) He never breaks His promises! When we, according to His will, sincerely seek, knock and ask, He will never fail to draw us nearer to Him. I suspect that even if the request was half- hearted, as in "God if you're really there…" He would still delight in making His presence known, because that is the kind of God He is.

God is Love and He wants all his little children to come near to Him. There are accounts in Matthew, Mark and Luke of the time He rebuked the adults and made it clear they should let the children come near to him. (Matthew 19:14, Mark 10:14 and Luke18:16) In those cases, Jesus was literally talking about the young children who had approached him, but we are still all His children and I'm sure I for one can be extremely annoying! When he said, "Let the little children come to me, and do not hinder them, for the kingdom of heaven belongs to such as these" (Matthew 19:14) wouldn't it make sense that he is extending this offer to every child, of every age, who longs to approach our Lord? I'm sure God loves it when we jostle ourselves in for a hug and better yet, when we stay there.

Unfortunately, as much as I love feeling God is beside me, I too often lose track of that awareness and when that happens, obedience can be a scary thing. With all the times God met me exactly where I was and provided in ways I couldn't have imagined possible, I would think that obedience to God would be the easiest thing in the world, but overthinking gets me in trouble. It's hard to have one foot on the planet and one in Heaven. Temptation is everywhere and sometimes it seems like it could be easy to justify an action that really is the opposite of what God wants from me. Thankfully prayer and His word work wonders in keeping God's children on track.

Often, just like Ana's story, I've been fearful of doing what I thought maybe I should; questioning whether this was really from God or whether I was making it up. I remember once years ago when I had taken my father in to emergency at the hospital. He was in the room being attended to and I had been asked to leave for a few minutes. As I stood out in the middle of the wing, I noticed a woman in the bed beside Dad's area. I wanted to ask if she'd like me to pray for her but I was nervous to approach. My head conversation went something like this. *I feel like I should go pray with her God, should I? Really Deb, you're not the saviour and besides she might not want some stranger approaching; but really God it can't ever be wrong to pray for someone, can it?; but what if she doesn't want me to? God if this is really from you, if you want me to go talk to her and pray with her please make it clear. By your power and in Jesus name please make it crystal clear!*

At that moment I glanced over at her, she looked me square in the eye and smiled. I took that as my cue, went over to her bedside and spoke with her briefly. I don't even remember what I said. Likely, it started with an introduction and a commiseration that I was sorry she was in the hospital. Then I asked, "Would it be okay for me to pray for you?" There was not a moment's hesitation on her part; she was grateful and so happy to have me pray for her. Not long after, her husband joined her and I went off to be with my dad. I don't know what happened to her but I have always been hopeful that she recovered from that episode. Even if she didn't, God worked on both our lives that day, encouraging me to step out in obedience even if it feels a little weird, and encouraging her with some measure of peace and joy when she was lying in that hospital bed. It was a gift for both of us!

So getting back to why I think my heart may be full today despite that element of sorrow at leaving my family and friends and that beautiful little granddaughter of ours; I must admit I was sorely tempted to stay behind. I could have; my husband suggested it first and a friend was willing to put me up. It would have been easy to justify but here's the thing. It didn't sit right. I had a niggling notion I was meant to leave for home, even if "home" doesn't quite feel that way yet. I truly sensed that my place should be with my husband. I didn't want him to drive the distance through the wintery mountain terrain alone and I didn't want him to come home to be alone for an undetermined amount of time while I stayed put in Calgary.

I also had to question my faith and trust in God's provision. Do I really walk the walk? Do I trust that God loves my family, especially our newest little member as much as we do - even more so - and that He will provide for our daughter, son-in-law and granddaughter in everything? He will give them strength for the transition and has already set up a beautiful day care situation for Evelyn with her other grandparents. Yes it means it will be harder on our daughter Stephanie and Evelyn with having to get up much earlier, dress and feed the baby and get them both out the door in the cold, dark mornings but God will give them strength and there will be huge blessings and benefits that come with it.

So here I am, back in our new home that hasn't even been fully organized. We moved from Victoria to Nanaimo at the end of last June and have been away twice, for a total of four months since we first arrived. There's lots of work to be done and a community to get to know but it feels good and it feels right. Why is that and how can I explain this profound sense of joy? It may just have something to do with the fact that I've had time to worship this morning; God filled my heart with gratitude and song; My Bible breathed more life into me as God reminded me of His faithfulness. He moved me forward despite some initial reluctance on my part. Though I didn't know where this morning's devotional writing would take me, God did. My heart is full; God is in this!

All I needed to do was step out; just as Abram and Sarai set out in obedience, not knowing where their journey would take them or what it would be like, and yet God blessed them miraculously. Today, God brought me where He needed me to be. It started with only a prayer, a Bible reading and a tiny step in the right direction – towards Him. I hope we will all be able to take that tiny step for all our todays and find peace, joy and abundant blessings in Him!

Holy Father,
Thank You for giving me opportunities to meet with You in prayer, in your word and in delightful fellowship with others! Forgive me for all the times I have been reluctant to move forward or been tempted to give up. Help me to always trust enough to take that first tiny step towards You and persevere in my endeavours to serve You. Let each tiny step be followed by many more. Please keep me close to You and continue to pour out your living water, saturating my soul and drawing me ever nearer to You! In Jesus Name I Pray.
Amen.

Ask and You Will Receive: Finding Answers in Scripture

Cloudburst, Mount Washington, Vancouver Island, British Columbia

© Bob Crosby

We were cross country skiing one late afternoon at Mt. Washington when we came upon this scene; a misty and slowly darkening tree lined meadow with a spectacularly beautiful cloud formation. Long thin rays of cloud stretched up before the sun. It made me pause and whimsically reflect that the golden scene before me could almost be God's Crown or a beautiful gateway into Heaven. I could have stared at it for ages but gave into my husband's wisdom that we'd better keep going to make sure we got back before dark.

Have you ever had moments that fill you with an almost unreasonable sense of joy and a kind of dance- like lightness in your mind and body when things are going incredibly well? Perhaps it was the day you first met Jesus, a peaceful beautiful moment alone or time spent with someone precious when you were so full of love and gratitude that you thought your heart might burst. That's what those rays of cloud over the sun did for me. I still have that sensation just thinking about them. They felt like a precious gift from God; as if He were saying 'Here you go; I just wanted to remind you how much I LOVE YOU. Enjoy my sovereign splendour and majesty; it's for you.'

It's for all of us, including you. I hope we will always be able to notice and experience the glory of God's creative beauty, hear the personal words He whispers to us through scripture and remember the depth of His love for each one!

"So they took Jesus in the boat and started out, leaving the crowds behind (although other boats followed.) But soon a fierce storm came up. High waves were breaking into the boat, and it began to fill with water.

Jesus was sleeping at the back of the boat with his head on a cushion. The disciples woke him up, shouting, "Teacher, don't you care that we're going to drown?"

When Jesus woke up, he rebuked the wind and said to the waves, "Silence! Be still!" Suddenly the wind stopped and there was a great calm. Then He asked them, "Why are you afraid? Do you still have no faith?"

The disciples were absolutely terrified. "Who is this man?" they asked each other. "Even the wind and waves obey him!" (Mark 4: 36- 41)

"What a mighty God we serve!" He is in our life boat with us and willing to take control, even if we have just a little faith; "Because you have so little faith. Truly I tell you, if you have faith as small as a mustard seed, you can say to this mountain, 'Move from here to there,' and it will move." (Matthew 17:20)

As I sat reading my Bible and praying during my devotional time this morning, God moved me to tears. There's a huge storm and a pretty big mountain that needs moving. Two Canadian men are being held prisoners in China and another young man incarcerated and accused of drug smuggling has been sentenced to death. However, there is mysterious power in prayer. What a gift that God calls us to join Him in Holy pursuits and has taught us to pray for others! I have prayed for these prisoners off and on since the news broke but today God made it more personal and more urgent. Right now the future for those men seems remarkably grim but I know that God miraculously released Paul from a prison long ago and I know He can release these men too. Thankfully our God is a God of miracles and remembering that gives hope to my prayers. He did it before; He can do it again if it is His will.

Heavenly Father; You still care and miracles still happen! Therefore "by prayer and petition and with thanksgiving" I ask: God, PLEASE, I hope it is in your good and perfect will to set these prisoners in China free! I pray that "They will soon be set free, they will not die in their dungeon, nor will they lack bread." (Isaiah 51: 14) I also pray for the Government and people of China, that You will meet them where they are and soften their hearts to experience your love, hope, mercy and peace. In Jesus Holy Name I Pray. Amen.

While thinking of these prisoners, God reminded me of another miracle that I was privileged to partner with Him in prayer for. It was during the Iraqi war. I heard the news that three American soldiers who were working on a road had been captured; two men and a woman. I'm sure many were concerned and praying for them; I had a very intense experience though. It's hard to explain but it was as if they were my own brothers and sister. For three nights I couldn't sleep and was consumed by thoughts of them. I prayed throughout those long nights over and over until by the end of the third night, I felt an unbelievable peace wash over me.

Before I continue, I should explain that in my morning Bible reading, I usually just start where I left off. My friend Rachel got me started years ago. As a new Christian, she told me to start with the New Testament first. I did and have just kept reading my way through the Bible since, along with some more directed reading for studies. It amazes me the way the Word truly is "living and breathing" and never fails to meet me where I'm at with my life journey. It met me then too!

On the fourth day, I happened to be in the book of Isaiah. As I was thinking of these soldiers and reading my Bible, a verse jumped off the page at me, crystal clear and speaking a beautiful promise;

"The cowering prisoners will soon be set free; they will not die in their dungeon, nor will they lack bread." (Isaiah 51:14)

I can't explain why I knew this was a personal promise but I did and I was ecstatic! I still kept praying for them and waiting to hear the news that they were free but God's idea of "soon" is sadly different than mine. I waited a number of months. I even heard from a friend who thought she heard they were dead. At that point I just gave it over. God, I thought I understood that you were going to free these soldiers but I guess there are two ways of freeing us, one on the planet and one at home with you.

It made me sad but I've been around long enough to realize that we don't always get the results from prayer that we were hoping for. I always trust that God knows what's best so have to acknowledge that my prayers may not be in line with His chosen outcome. It seemed this situation was one of those times. I prayed for comfort, peace and strength for their families and my life continued.

A few months later I was chaperoning our son's high school band trip from Calgary to Victoria. I came down to the bus with my group of girls one morning to be met by a gentleman who was also chaperoning the band. Almost the first words out of his mouth were "Did you hear the news today?"

"No I haven't; what's up?"

"Well, you know those soldiers that were captured in Iraq? They've been found!"

"The three that were working on the road?"

"Yes."

"Are they okay? What about the helicopter crew?" Very shortly after they went missing members of a downed helicopter crew were also captured and had been added to my prayers.

"Yes, they were in a group found together. They are all okay."

Just writing this brings me back to the awe of that moment. Not only did God keep His promise to free the prisoners, He made sure I knew it! What are the odds that with all the stories on the news that morning, and all the adults on the trip, he would come directly to me and this would be the news story that was reported? I was so overwhelmed by God's goodness and was thrilled to be able to tell that gentleman and a number of others how God had made that promise and made sure I knew He delivered on it.

Then, one Easter week our daughter and I drove to Vancouver Island from Calgary to see my father who was very ill in hospital. It had been difficult to see him looking so frail and wasted. He had been put on very strong narcotics by his attending doctor, and his mind was also frail. It was an emotional time when we had to say goodbye and once more I struggled a little. I was ridiculously reluctant to pray aloud over him; fearing what - that I'd offend someone maybe? I don't know why I hesitate sometimes. Most of the people I've met, believers or not, faced with ill health or fearful circumstances, have expressed a desire and gratitude for prayer.

Fortunately, that particular weekend, God faithfully moved me to pray; not only for Dad but for those nurses, doctors and staff attending him and the other patients in his room. I was tearful when I left to catch the ferry. As we waited at the terminal, God met me with another promise in His word and I absolutely knew that God would heal my dad. Since it was Easter Monday, I was reading through the gospel accounts of the resurrection. In the book of Mark, I came to this passage: "He (Jesus) said to them, 'Go into all the world and preach the good news to all creation. Whoever believes and is baptized will be saved, but whoever does not believe will be condemned. And these signs will accompany those who believe: In my name they will drive out demons; they will speak in new tongues; they will pick up snakes with their hands; and when they drink deadly poison, it will not hurt them at all; they will place their hands on sick people and they will get well." (Mark 16: 15-18) I recoiled at the thought of people picking up snakes and drinking poison, but when I read that last "sign" my heart leapt. Once more, though I couldn't explain why, I just knew that was God's promise to me at that very moment. He had heard my prayers and would send us another Easter miracle. God would heal my earthly father in this lifetime on this planet and He did!

Getting back to the idea of handling snakes and drinking poison especially when Jesus Himself being tested in the wilderness answered, "It is said: 'Do not put the Lord your God to the test.'" (Luke 4:12) We know God is more than able to protect, but why would we deliberately put ourselves in harm's way when Jesus and His Holy Word taught us not to!

I have often read scriptures wanting the outcome of a personal situation to be the same as the verses seemed to be suggesting but not sure it would. It's not that I doubted God's power. It's because I doubted whether I was praying in His will. Maybe God has better plans for that person than staying on Earth any longer. Who am I to say? There have been times I've prayed fervently for healing, once for a friend's young son battling leukemia, fully believing in a miracle for Sheldon and yet God took Him home; answering our prayers for healing just not in the way we'd hoped for.

While Bible verses don't always sound like a personal answer to my prayers, occasionally specific verses have thrilled me to my core and I've been totally confident of the outcome. Being with God like that and experiencing those moments makes me want to keep coming back to His word daily. It is always a blessing to read His word, but then there are those extra special moments with God that have provided insanely personal messages. They leave me breathless with the wonder of His love; "When I consider your heavens, the work of your fingers, the moon and the stars, which you have set in place, what is mankind that you are mindful of them, human beings that you care for them? You have made them a little lower than the angels and crowned them with glory and honor. You made them rulers over the works of your hands; you put everything under their feet: all flocks and herds, and the animals of the wild, the birds in the sky, and the fish in the sea, all that swim the paths of the seas. LORD, our LORD, how majestic is your name in all the earth!"(Psalm 8:3-9)

Holy Father

Thank You for all the times You meet us in your word with a very personal response to our concerns or circumstances. Forgive me for the times that I have forgotten and been distracted by foolish pursuits. Thank You for your gracious forgiveness! Thank You too for the love, mercy and miracles You send into our lives that help us to know You better and trust in your faithfulness! Let me never forget all the times You have blessed us miraculously. By your Holy Spirit power please send out your rays of hope; penetrate all the world's darkness with the brilliance of your love and light; and keep us close to You for You alone are worthy of praise!

In Jesus Name.

Amen.

God's Got This - Even When it Seems Like He Doesn't!

Milky Way – Abel Tasman Park, New Zealand © Bob Crosby

There's just something about nature that can stir deep gratitude for the incredible beauty God created on our behalf! It can be as sweeping as the Milky Way, mountain summits, glorious sunsets or the play of sunlight's beams on blue water that dance on the waves.

Sometimes though it can be a tiny flower, brilliant fall leaf, or shimmering insect that catches my eye. It's in those tiny beauties that I can become even more overwhelmed with gratitude for God's artistic attention to detail. As much as I love and appreciate the beauty my gratitude is not just because of their visual appeal. In part it is because of the recognition of how perfectly useful God made each molecule; all of nature meshes and works together to the benefit of His creatures. The exquisite little item before me presents a minute fraction of the scientific systems He so gloriously created for us all, right down to the microscopic cells in our bodies and the systems that keep us alive. Some think it a great accident and coincidence this planet with all its living growing inhabitants came into being but I can't imagine it that way. It is far too perfect to be some primordial accident.

If God did all this for us, how could we ever doubt His faithfulness? Life is fragile. All the prayers for healing for loved ones don't always lead to the outcome we most desire; healing on this planet. Like all those gorgeous fall leaves, tender flower blooms and luminescent bugs, we too will only live on this Earth for our God- ordained season. However, thanks to Jesus' free, grace-filled gift of salvation, we know we will pass beyond this Earth and into His presence. It is really only there that we will experience perfect healing. There is such comfort, peace, hope and gratitude knowing that He's got this; and it is and will be beautiful!

"Soon afterward, Jesus went to a town called Nain, and his disciples and a large crowd went along with Him. As he approached the town gate, a dead person was being carried out-the only son of his mother, and she was a widow. And a large crowd from the town was with her. When the LORD saw her, his heart went out to her and he said, "Don't cry." Then he went up and touched the bier they were carrying him on, and the bearers stood still. He said, "Young man, I say to you, get up!" The dead man sat up and began to talk, and Jesus gave him back to his mother. They were all filled with awe and praised God. "A great prophet has appeared among us," they said. "God has come to help his people." This news about Jesus spread throughout Judea and the surrounding country." (Luke 7: 11-17)

In the late 1970's, I was working on the "Thousand Islanders" tour boats out of Gananoque, Ontario. We were a relatively closely knit crew who enjoyed each other's company on and off work hours. Just for context, I need to let you know that Rex was one of the crew who was pretty popular with everyone.

During an evening off, instead of meeting with some of my boat line friends I took the bus from Gananoque to Kingston to see a production of Godspell. I boarded with Mrs. Bilton over the summers I worked there, and that year her son was playing in the orchestra. Live theatre would be a treat and it seemed like a good idea to support John too.

That night as we rolled along the highway back to Gananoque I was looking out the bus window enjoying the scenery. I'd enjoyed the music and the play; now the lush Ontario countryside fringed by a gloriously golden sunset was picture perfect. Quite suddenly something was inexplicably wrong. For no apparent reason, an overwhelming sense of dread came over me. It was almost as if I was being draped in a black shroud; the sensation was tangible and my fear seemed to penetrate deep within. I don't remember if I prayed. At that time I was more of a seeker; I believed in God but hadn't really met Jesus and didn't pray all that often. Even so, as suddenly as it had descended on me the dread was replaced with another almost deeper sense of warmth and peace. I could have sworn that I heard clearly, "*Don't worry Debbie, it will be okay.*" Everything was right in my world and everything would be fine. It was such a strong wave of peace that broke over the fear and dread, that it left me thrilled by the comfort of its promise.

I returned back to my landlady's home and climbed Mrs. Bilton's stairs, smiling yet puzzled by this strange experience. I was less confident now. Was it just an overactive imagination, spurred on by the evening's entertainment that was playing tricks on me on that bus? Soon I crawled into bed and slept.

The next morning when I arrived at the dock for work we were all shaken up with the news our lovely boss Jean delivered; "Rex was in a terrible accident last night. He's in bad shape in the hospital." The night before wasn't wasted on me. I was sure it was God preparing me with a promise that everything would turn out okay in the end. Rex would recover. I knew it.

Around noon as we pulled into the dock, I threw the bow line out to the deckhand and as he wrapped it around the post to secure it, I saw Jean, hurriedly approaching. She looked upset and I called out to her. "Jean, how's Rex, have you heard?"

I'll never forget her look. She was wide eyed and tearful as she approached. "Rex is dead."

I was devastated. I was so sure God had promised me; even though I didn't know at the time what the promise was about, He made it clear that *everything would be alright. How could this be? Not Rex*!

There wasn't a dry eye with our crew on that next sailing. The poor passengers must have wondered what was going on as they boarded the ship to be greeted by a red eyed, sometimes sobbing crew. We did our best to welcome them but none of us were in great shape to be working.

I don't remember how much time passed, maybe twenty minutes, maybe much longer. The captain called down to the concession stand from the wheelhouse. I picked up his phone expecting a request for coffee or a cold drink. Instead he said "Debbie, Rex isn't dead." Silence – my head wasn't getting it.

"Debbie, He's not dead!"

"You're kidding?" (As if anyone would kid about that! I felt stupid the moment it came out.)

"No, Rex isn't dead. The hospital made a mistake. We just got the call over the radio."

Now the tourists on board must really have wondered what was happening. Suddenly we were all laughing and crying. It was a moment we never could have imagined. Hospitals don't make mistakes like that!

It was one of the most emotional days of my young life. I went on to University and didn't see much of the old town and crew after that, but I heard that Rex did very well with his long slow healing process; a gift from God and a lot of hard work by Rex. I wish I'd stayed in touch with all the crew over the years. I can't help but think God spared Rex for something really special. I'd like to know how he used that gift.

I'm humbled when I think of how quickly I was ready to believe that God didn't keep his promise. Ever notice how even non-believers criticize God when things are going poorly, such as "If God is all you say He is, He wouldn't allow this to happen!"

When Jean told me Rex was dead, my immediate instinct was that God let me down. *This isn't alright God*! Yet He knew it was and may have smiled; the same way many parents might smile when they know something wonderful and anticipate revealing that special surprise to their kids. Perhaps God smiles every time He amazes us with the miracles of delivering on His promises. Maybe this isn't just because our impossible prayers are answered and He has used our trial to bring us closer to Him. Maybe it's born out of the bigger miracle of His deep love for us.

Isn't it amazing that our God could love us with such tenderness and mercy that He would reach down from Heaven to look after His children? That in the same way "His heart went out to" the woman who had lost her son, His heart goes out to each of us comforting us through our hardships with His divine love.

What loving parent fails to find joy when he or she has been able to help a child overcome a hurdle? Sometimes though, parents realize it is a hurdle their child had to jump over alone. No matter how difficult the circumstance and how great our desire to bail out our kids; perhaps do some of their homework project for them or have a difficult conversation on their behalf, we realize that sometimes the best thing we can do for them is equip and encourage them to handle it themselves. God must be thrilled to see us rejoice when He guides us through the quick sand of our hardships, lifts us up and puts us back down on His solid ground, stronger and more able to meet the next challenge!

Though God has complete power and could easily remove our difficulties, I trust He knows what is best and it is from a place of love that He allows me/us to walk through them. It has taken me a long time to cultivate that trust and especially to learn to listen to the Holy Spirit's leading. I'm still working on it! I remember times when I could sense I shouldn't "go" or "do" or "say" but walked on into the mud because I failed to listen and respond to His direction. I'm so grateful that He never let go of me despite my lack of faithful obedience! It is such a blessing to think on the miracle of God's love. "The LORD your God is with you, He is mighty to save. He will take great delight in you, He will quiet you with his love, He will rejoice over you with singing."(Zephaniah 3:17)
Sometimes it's hard to imagine that despite all our flaws He "delights in His children." We may have ignored Him for years, behaved grievously or even doubted His existence yet He so

faithfully and willingly comes to us, comforts, encourages and illuminates our way through any patches of darkness we encounter. He's got us; it's true! All we need to do is ask Him.

Sovereign Father,

Thank You for being our faithful God; for sending your Holy Spirit to teach us and your precious son Jesus Christ to take our place on the cross!
Please make us all eager and willing to praise You in all things; and quickly turn to You for your guidance and help to deal with every trial we encounter in life. Let us always remember to give thanks, even in our darkest moments for You have promised to "work all things for the good of those who love You" and your promises never fail. Forgive us for the times we have tried to barrel ahead without You! Please fill us up to overflowing with peace, joy and complete trust in You; and when your answers seem slow to come or different than an outcome we'd hoped and prayed for, don't let us despair. Let us trust in Jesus Name!

Thank You Lord!

Amen.

God of Mercy

Wedge Pond, Kananaskis, Alberta © Bob Crosby

Like the golden reflection of trees and mountains on still water, God's love and mercy comes down and rests over us. We need but open our hearts and eyes to see His love and blessings all around us. We have never been alone in any of our trials, even though we may have felt that way. Though circumstances in our lives may seem as immovable as a mountain, and our pathway through the problem blocked by a thick dark forest, we need not fear. God's "word is a lamp onto my feet and a light onto my path." (Psalm 119:105) "The LORD himself goes before you and will be with you; He will never leave you nor forsake you. Do not be afraid; do not be discouraged."(Deuteronomy 31:8)

The beauty of this scene, reflected in the crystal clear mountain waters seems to me a breathtaking reminder that God is not only above me but all around me, reflecting His deep love and faithfulness in a way that nothing else can.

I remember the day we were there quite vividly, though it was many years ago. It was such a still and gloriously clear fall morning. We'd ridden our bikes from a campground past open vistas with inspiring mountain views and through tree lined trails of gold and green. More of God's glory was revealed with every peddle we took along that path. When we got to the pond, we left our bikes at the top and made our way down the path drinking in the golden beauty of the trees and the rugged giants standing tall against a brilliant sky. They were surrounding us in creation's grand embrace and reflecting it back in the glassy bright blue of the pond. Not even a ripple could be found and we had the whole incredible scene to ourselves, at least for a little while. Isn't God's love like that; nothing to muddy it, just pure, bright, and crystal clear pouring down on us from above and reflecting back from us when we let it! It is a gift for all and yet it is also intensely personal; just one on one, this Father's love for you!

" Have mercy on me, O God,
   according to your unfailing love;
according to your great compassion
   blot out my transgressions.
Wash away all my iniquity
   and cleanse me from my sin.
For I know my transgressions,
   and my sin is always before me.
Against you, you only, have I sinned
   and done what is evil in your sight;
so you are right in your verdict
   and justified when you judge.
Surely I was sinful at birth,
   sinful from the time my mother conceived me.
Yet you desired faithfulness even in the womb;
   you taught me wisdom in that secret place.
Cleanse me with hyssop, and I will be clean;
   wash me, and I will be whiter than snow.
Let me hear joy and gladness;
   let the bones you have crushed rejoice.
Hide your face from my sins
   and blot out all my iniquity.
Create in me a pure heart, O God,
   and renew a steadfast spirit within me.

Do not cast me from your presence
   or take your Holy Spirit from me.
Restore to me the joy of your salvation
   and grant me a willing spirit, to sustain me." (Psalm 51:1-12)

As I sit at my desk, the window in front of me is vying for my attention. It's snowing on the west coast! This is not a frequent occurrence here and being from back east it is to my great delight. I love snow!

I remember those moments as a child when we'd awake to a flurry of white. We'd be overjoyed with excitement, especially with the first snowfall of the season. I couldn't wait to get breakfast over with, and for Mom to help us dress with all those layers and thick bulky snowsuits so we could get out into it. By the time we finally had all our gear on we looked more like colourful versions of well-padded snowmen or astronauts on a spacewalk than kids sent off to play. It felt like we could barely move at first, but we did and we'd have a wonderful time building snowmen, making snow angels and as we got a little older, pretending we were arctic explorers.

I still feel excited when I see a multitude of unique and glorious flakes falling from the sky; though I'm not always so happy if I have to drive in it. Then it can become frightening unless I give my anxiety over to God.

That is not to say that I would risk driving in a storm if I didn't need to; but I have some wonderful verses that calm my spirit whenever I dwell on them. I committed these verses to memory many years if not decades ago and I like to pray them into my life whenever I'm worried about anything. Though these verses were mentioned earlier I think they bear repeating in the context of making them a prayer: Lord let me "Rejoice in (You) Always. I will say it again: Rejoice! Let my gentleness be evident to all. (You are) near. (Let me) not be anxious about anything, but in (this and in) every situation, by prayer and petition, with thanksgiving, (let me) present (my) requests to (You). And (You oh Lord,) the God of peace that transcends all understanding, will guard (my) heart and mind in Christ Jesus." (Philippians 4: 4-7) Thank you that **You are** guarding my "heart and mind" in Jesus!

It blesses me beyond description every time I pray these verses and think on His promise that my "heart and mind are being guarded in Christ Jesus!" I have never once been let down with this prayer. My circumstances rarely have changed but the peace of God has always come flooding in like a high tide in the Bay of Fundy. It washes over me and removes the trouble and fear that had been invading my mind. Sometimes the peace came instantly; other times I had to wrestle with that prayer multiple times to find it, but it always came even if the circumstances stayed the same!

I mentioned earlier that "calm" was not something I am especially good at and it was even worse when I was younger. I have experienced a few situations that really rattled me and one especially that left me with a high level of anxiety and the occasional panic attack. Our kids were young and I was mostly a stay at home mother but took a part time job at a new grocery store that opened up nearby us so I could help my husband with our family expenses. One particular night a co-worker asked "Debbie, would you mind trading and going on the express till. I'm really tired."

I was happy to help her out as I liked the quick pace, especially late at night to keep me awake and alert. What I didn't know as I moved to the till was that the third person through my line would look at me with an enormous scowl, throw something over the counter at me and say "fill it!" I was studying the item. It looked a lot like a sheet that had been covered in silver duct tape but it had a lot of numbers and letters in orderly print. I was about to call a supervisor thinking that it was some kind of new voucher I hadn't seen, when I looked up to see his hand go behind his shirt and a gun come out and point at me. Then I understood what I needed to do!

We had been trained, "don't be heroes!" I had two young children and a husband at home waiting for me so I didn't have any trouble with that direction. I started shoving money into his pouch. The cash drawer was emptied. He growled at me "Lift the drawer!" It was here we often kept a couple of large bills along with cheques and paper stubs from credit or debit card transactions. When I had stuffed in all I had, he reached his empty hand towards me. "Give it here!" As I was handing the bag to him a five dollar bill fell out. I was desperately trying to push it back in, fearful that he would pull the trigger, but he just yelled "that's enough" grabbed the bag and ran.

It was a very strange and traumatic experience. I've heard of people "leaving their bodies" and it felt a bit like that. I felt like I was looking down on me and the situation from above. I remember the clips holding down the bills in my tray looking enormous to me and feeling like I was struggling to lift them. My hands looked and felt extra large, heavy, and slow moving. Despite my sense of urgency and desire to hurry, I was more like a robot motoring slowly and methodically through my job. I was frightened and praying fiercely, but at the same time the observer in me felt oddly calm. Once he was through the doors I called the store code over the intercom. I had enough presence of mind to stop my manager running after him with the shout. "NO STOP! He has a gun!"

It was quite late; about 11:45 at night and only 15 minutes before the end of my shift.
I stood calmly at my till until one of my coworkers came over to me and asked if I was alright. Then I fell to pieces and started to sob, being physically supported and escorted past a handful of staring customers and up into the safety of the office. In only a few minutes the police had arrived but their interview would take longer.

I don't remember how long I was there. I do remember my boss kindly offering to drive me home. I was in no shape to get behind the wheel. Once home to my sleeping family I was a mess. I hated to wake Bob when work came so early but I felt desperate. Bob is a light sleeper so crawling into bed and hoping for a response I whispered "Are you awake?" As soon as he replied in the affirmative, my emotions let loose and I began to sob again. He held and comforted me as I replayed the evening's events.

I was home with my kids that morning and so grateful but also still terribly frightened and worried that I would see the man who did it; that he would recognize me and come after me. I closed my blinds and huddled in the house. This fear I learned later is a common response by victims.

I was trying so hard to act like it was a normal day for our kids but inside I felt like I could barely function. I called our dear friend Rachel, just wanting another adult to talk to. Despite Rachel's move out of our town and a significant drive away she insisted she come in and be with me. I'm still so grateful to her and her husband Bill for that gift! It helped me and our kids through that difficult day. Multiple panic attacks came later and I am also thankful for counselling sessions with incredibly skilled and compassionate women; and to Safeway for making that possible. Incidentally Rachel later went back to school and became a counsellor. She is still exercising her God given passion and talents to help many who are struggling with life!

The wonderful thing about it all though, was that even during my struggles with anxiety I could see how God had put the right person at that till. The lady I relieved was exhausted and hadn't made a cash drop for quite some time. The bills were so thick under the clips that with my first two transactions I dropped literally hundreds of dollars in the lock box below our till. She also was younger and more nervous. I am a very visual person so I was maybe able to give a clearer description to the police and I definitely was able to identify him with police photos. Once I identified him, the officers told me they thought he was the thief and he was "well known to them for supporting his habit."

I also wondered if I hadn't moved tills, if my friend may have screamed and been shot. Though I had no idea about her level of faith, at least I was able to pray throughout the ordeal. God was faithful. He got me through it and though it took a long time to fully recover, I haven't had a panic attack for at least ten years.

It was ultimately a more painful struggle that brought me final healing from this episode. When our daughter entered her mid-teens she became sullen and distant from me. It broke my heart, especially since I had always been close to my mother and one of my biggest goals in life was to be a good parent. At that time in my life we pretty much had no relationship. I would greet her in the morning as I always had and she would glare back at me silently. Conversation was at a bare minimum. One day I was frustrated and trying to relay that I understood things were hard, but… I don't remember the words I spoke but they were a bad idea. No one's problem is ever the same as what we have gone through and stating it with frustration just makes things worse! It was a very poor call on my part and certainly not validating. I could not know, nor could I understand. Stephanie was emphatically stating "you have no idea!" She lifted her pant leg to reveal that she had cut the word "sorrow" into her leg. It was devastating! As I so often do, I blamed myself, though for years after she tried to tell me "it's not your fault Mom."

Still, good parents build relationships with their children; they talk about problems and work them out. I felt I had failed her. I could only bring it before God's throne of grace and seek help for our tearful daughter. My husband's workplace fortunately provided benefits for counselling. We went to a few sessions with one counsellor who made it abundantly clear that Stephanie's problems were all because of me, as she literally closed the door in my face. Again, I heard and believed the oppressor's lies blaming me for everything that was wrong for my family. I felt utterly useless and ashamed of the kind of parent I had become.

God was in that too. A couple of sessions in and Stephanie didn't want to go back to see my accuser. I started asking around and found another counsellor, who treated us with equal respect and helped us both. In the course of the sessions, when Stephanie complained of my over protectiveness and mentioned the hold up, Carrie learned of my experience. She recommended I try EMDR therapy. I read up on it and was a little worried about the possible negative side effects but decided it was worth a try. It has been known to cause nightmares for some but euphoria for others. I learned something of great interest from our counsellor. When we experience a traumatic event, our brain waves arrange themselves in a particular way and anytime we think of that episode again our brain waves are always in exactly the same pattern. With EMDR therapy, while being questioned about the episode in a safe and relaxed environment by my trained counsellor; and receiving very light shocks from small paddles in my hands, my brain wave patterns were changed. This apparently has been a useful treatment for some PTSD sufferers and it certainly helped me overcome the panic attacks. More importantly Carrie also provided much needed help to Stephanie.

It took a number of more years to grow a little closer and it still often feels like baby steps. I know she loves me but sometimes it feels like she doesn't like me. I seem to have a knack for irritating her, but am grateful God is working on us and our relationship is getting better.

It wasn't until Stephanie was well into her twenties that she revealed she had been sexually molested when she was only about 5 or 6 years old by an older girl living beside us. I was sickened by her news. It was one of the dangers I'd most wanted to protect her from since I had also experienced a couple of brief encounters with molestation by strangers as a young teen. Once was on a school field trip to a cave where our very large guide stepped in front of me and positioned himself in a narrow opening, leering at me as I was forced to follow the single file and turn sideways to squeeze past him. Another time was while I was watching a parade with my parents and younger siblings. Someone behind me had their hand exploring up the back of my blouse for a good part of the parade. I should have said something but I was frozen and simply kept my arms squeezed against my sides with all my might. I felt so dirty but I wouldn't dare cause a scene. Almost from day one, we'd been taught to be kind. No matter what, we must never hurt someone else's feelings! Far be it from me to do otherwise.

That sure wouldn't happen today! I've learned since that many abusers have an uncanny ability to pick their victims knowing that they wouldn't speak out. God help me; I will never be a victim again and I pray the same for our kids and grandkids; present and future!

Now I learned that Stephanie was a victim and once more I felt like a huge failure. I was home when it was happening! I wondered why the neighbour spent so much time playing with a girl at least two years younger than her, but it seemed that her family were a little isolated and rarely spent time socializing with anyone other than their extended family. I'd take her to the park with us or arrange a family picnic with her parents and sisters. I just thought she was lonely. They had lived there for a significant amount of time and the children hadn't even been to the nearby park. They all seemed like good people and I was completely blind to this girl's treatment of our daughter. I do remember being concerned when our happy go lucky girl with great giggles and joy became more quiet and serious. I even asked her then, "Stephanie is everything okay? You don't seem as happy. Did anything happen that you want to tell me about?" She didn't and it continued.

Meanwhile our son Michael was battling depression and anxiety. It was just starting to surface and again my guilt was alive and well. When he was a toddler, we lived in Richmond, B.C. and I'd established friendships with other young moms. We'd often get together and let the kids play. Michael was a social, outgoing happy little boy. Then we moved. We bought a house in Surrey, the only affordable community near Vancouver within commuting distance for my husband. We still got together with our friends but much less frequently. On top of that we now had his new baby sister vying for attention. I managed to enroll Mike in special programs a couple of times a week but my heart ached for my joyful outgoing little boy who was becoming much more serious. I tried to find a child to babysit but the only respondents to my advertisement needed day care for their infants. I needed a playmate for my toddler and other than scheduled programs I couldn't find one.

Over the years Mike had a few tough transitions. We also had to move to take the job in Calgary just as he was entering junior high. All the kids in our new neighbourhood were Stephanie's age or older than Mike. He spent way too much time playing video games instead of being with friends. I was so concerned about him sitting at home alone and playing video games, I did something radical. I prayed and I asked my friends from a Mothers Who Care group who pray for local schools, kids and staff to pray with me for my kids. Then at age 14, we told Mike he had to get a job to help fund his upcoming band trip. I knew the grocery store near us would hire 14 year olds as service clerks. Fourteen is terribly young to go to work and we would have been able to pay for his trip but he didn't need to know that. I just wanted him to be out interacting with others and hoped he might make friends with someone at the store.

Mike started working. About the same time he started managing better at school. Mike had suffered a fair bit of bullying in the past. We'd got both the kids into Taekwondo classes hoping it would help keep them more fit and improve their self-esteem. One particular day when all the teachers were in a meeting after school two of his tormentors grabbed our son and started writing all over him. Mike had taken enough. He slammed the one kid into a locker and put the other into a headlock. Then let them go and walked away. Mike told me about it when he got home from school and I went immediately back to the school to speak with his vice principal. I was livid that those kids would treat our son that way and I was shaking. Once I overcame my tears, I told the vice principal exactly what I had said, "Though we always maintained he must never use violence, I told him "Good for you Mike; sometimes you need to stand up to the bullies." The vice principal understood this mother's heart and I will always be grateful for his wisdom and caring. He managed to deal with the problem so that all three boys came out with a sense of dignity and a sense of being understood. The problem was resolved and as far as this mother knows, he didn't have any more episodes of bullying at junior high.

I am convinced that it was only by prayer and God's faithfulness that God turned our kids' lives around. He gave Mike and Stephanie both musical talent and being in the band with fantastic teachers and conductors during junior and high school gave them a whole community of fellow "nerds" (in their words) to support and encourage each other.

However, Mike's depression and anxiety hit an all-time peak after graduating from college while he was working as a radio broadcaster in the tiny town of Chetwynd, B.C. I was aching for him and all I could do, but arguably the best I could do, was to pray for him. Of course connecting by phone may have provided some relief too. Fortunately we spoke frequently. He also recognized his problem and sought medical help. Praise God there was a doctor in Chetwynd who saw Mike quickly and got him onto medication for the depression. Mike had been so isolated and didn't have the strength to look after himself. He had free access to a gym but couldn't bring himself to go and work out where there were other people. Mike had also packed on a lot of weight and along with prayers for him to overcome the depression and anxiety, for at least a couple of years I had been praying for him to be able to make healthy choices to care for himself and get fit. As a teenager and young adult I'd been an overweight couch potato myself. Never athletic or popular, my pleasure was found escaping into books or TV and munching my way through life. I felt Mike's pain and I wanted him to be able to overcome it.

Soon after seeing the doctor and starting his medication, Mike reached out on social media and made a commitment to get healthy. He was met with a shower of encouragement from family and friends. He lost his job up north and returned to his support network in Calgary. There he continued to look after himself and decided that he would like to become a personal trainer so he could help others like himself. He took the course, became certified and is now happily working at a gym, when it isn't closed due to the pandemic and offering training to a number of clients. I'm so grateful that he understands their challenges and can offer empathy and encouragement along with his expertise. We don't get as many calls from him anymore. A couple of months ago after Mike hung up from a phone call my husband's response was "He sounds so happy, and so mature!" Bob was right and I felt a huge sense of relief and joy wash over me. Depression and anxiety has the potential to creep back in, but I'm grateful for the strides in medical science that have provided medication to help those who suffer; and for God's generosity in listening and answering our prayers for those who struggle with such illness.

I'm sharing these stories with the permission of our kids in the hopes that they may encourage others to know you are not alone. When my sister used to quip "our family puts the "fun" in "dysfunctional," I could relate! I so wanted to be that perfect wife and mother, protector, cheerleader, and parent provider with a healthy, joyful family life but I hadn't managed it.

Motherhood was a huge blessing but I had been cut down to my innermost being and I needed God to stop the bleeding and heal the wound. At that time in my life it felt like all the dreams and goals I'd had to raise a healthy, happy family couldn't have been farther from the truth. That was my problem. I foolishly thought **I** could. I was prideful; blind to the fact that I needed God to help me parent. I so wish I had learned earlier and been closer to God in those young years of parenting; prayed more and fretted less, asked for wisdom and discernment, had it revealed to me, listened and acted on it! I might have spared my daughter from such abuse and my son from such depression and anxiety. Yet, God healed me and blessed our kids. Despite my foolishness, God overcame the circumstances, my poor choices, bad calls and weak prayers and continues to bless my family in and through life's big challenges.

God has forgiven me and has graciously revealed another truth. I have to trust that while God doesn't cause such pain to happen, He sometimes allows it and uses it to bless others. Later on, Stephanie became a gifted and giving leader, mentoring the young people in her church. I suspect there wasn't much they could be going through that Stephanie hadn't already experienced and she was able to offer words of hope and encouragement to help many other young people. She has been able to honour God and overcome the abuse! When I asked her if she was able to forgive that girl, Stephanie replied in the affirmative telling me that something terrible must have happened in the girl's life for her to even think of doing such a thing. I can't imagine such forgiveness being humanly possible. Only God could give Stephanie that compassionate ability to recognize the perpetrator was broken herself and forgive her.

If you had told me five years ago that Mike would be working in a gym as a personal trainer I probably would have wondered what planet you were from. Now I am delighted and grateful that he is trying to look after himself, building a tool kit to help with the difficult times and that because of the struggles he had, he is so much more able to identify with and help those who are struggling the same way! More recently he has found the strength to go back to school and pursue another dream. It will be a long haul but I'm hopeful for him. I'll keep praying!

I am so proud of our kids and the way they stayed strong and were able to overcome the nightmares that faced them. Such tough life circumstances can bring conflict and anxiety. I have often struggled to hold onto the peace of God. I absolutely trust that God is there and could help me in any circumstance; I just sometimes struggle with whether or not He wants to. *Have I sinned one time too many with disobedience or simply ignoring Him and now I'm going to pay the price? Did I go ahead of Him and so now I can just wallow in whatever muck I got myself into? Has His love for me waned? Has He hardened His heart towards me?*

Even today I woke up with such thoughts. I was praying for people and in the midst of my prayers had very critical thoughts towards someone I was in the midst of praying for. *How could I Lord! How could I be in conversation with you and be so sinfully critical? It is the height of egotistical arrogance! How dare I judge someone else's motives? How can you keep forgiving me when I am so sinful? Oh please forgive me!*

What amazes me always is how He meets me in that very moment. *The answer is easy: Jesus took care of it on that cross. He paid the price for you and for all! It was and is "finished*!" He keeps forgiving because that's what God does. I had no sooner uttered my request than I was enveloped in peace. God was with me and He still loved me. He extended His unfathomable mercy and grace to cover me and made sure I understood what He had done.

Then just to reinforce it, God led me to reread a passage I read just yesterday in my Prayer Devotional Bible. (Max Lucado, Zondervan Corporation, 2004). I don't generally reread devotional passages a day after I've seen them. Though I do revisit them as I return to those sections in my Bible, I'm usually more motivated to get back into the scriptures. Today though, I was compelled to take a second look.

I'm so glad I did. I don't think I got it the first time through. It felt like a letter straight from God telling me He still loved me and yes, I'm forgiven! In this reading, Max Lucado was speaking of the account of the time a leper approached Jesus and said "Lord, if you are willing you can make me clean." (Luke 5: 12) First off, lepers didn't approach anyone. It was illegal to do so. As Lucado so eloquently stated, "…this account of the leper is more than a story about the healing of a diseased man; it is also a metaphor. The disease of leprosy stands for all that separates people from God and makes them unfit to be in his presence…and if we think God is disgusted by what he sees inside, we're less likely to pray. If that's you watch what Jesus does with this leper: He touched this untouchable and said," I am willing. Be clean!" (Luke 5: 13) Taken from the prayer Bible by Max Lucado © 2004 by The Zondervan Corporation. Used by permission of Zondervan. www.zondervan.com

I wonder at the joy that had to be the leper's at that moment. Just to be lovingly touched by another human being would have been an incredible gift, especially after who knows how long since he had been allowed human contact. Then, to be completely healed is an overwhelming testimony to the power of God in the person of Jesus Christ; and the incredible depth of His love. The leper had been given more than he could have asked for or imagined; "Now to Him who is able to do immeasurably more than all we ask or imagine, according to His power that is at work within us, to Him be glory in the church and in Christ Jesus throughout all generations, for ever and ever! Amen."(Ephesians 3:20)

That leper had been touched and healed. I can barely imagine how he must have felt; such indescribable joy at such miraculous, unbelievably good fortune! Yet, that is a little of what I felt like this morning when God reminded me in all His glory that His love for me (and you) never fades and we are always welcome in the arms of Jesus!

As impure, filthy, critical, egotistical or self-serving as my thoughts, words or actions ever are or ever could have been, His grace is enough! Whenever we turn to Him and ask, God's sublime gifts of love, mercy, peace and grace wrap around and layer over us like the snow suits of our youth. He holds us tight to protect us and keep us as pure, white and as peaceful as those fine flakes of snow falling from the sky.

When we reflect on His word, remembering His incredible gift of salvation, all the precious promises and gifts he has bestowed on us; or contemplate all the times that God has been so powerfully present in our circumstances, even times when we weren't aware of it, we are truly blessed. In his own struggles, Paul reflected on his trials and need for God; "Therefore, in order to keep me from becoming conceited, I was given a thorn in my flesh, a messenger of Satan, to torment me. Three times I pleaded with the LORD to take it away from me. But He said to me, "My grace is sufficient for you, for my power is made perfect in weakness."(2 Corinthians 12: 7-9)

In good and challenging times it is always best to go to God with thanksgiving and requests but I imagine it is even more crucial in our times of struggle and despair. I was as ashamed of my critical thoughts this morning as I was with the times I felt I failed as a parent. In fact I was inclined to leave out these stories because I wasn't sure I wanted you to know about what I perceived as my failings. How foolish! How can we encourage each other if we're not willing to be vulnerable and transparent? Perhaps it would have been easier for me too, if I'd pretended that God wasn't there this morning, or in the past, so that I wouldn't have had to face Him; at least not for now. We'll all have to face Him eventually. I'm so grateful though that I turned to Him first! Otherwise I might have missed the comfort and love He lavishly doled out to my family and myself through my times with Him; His message of hope and healing right down to this morning's gift when He extravagantly filled my west coast world with the creative beauty of His snow; His generous and gentle reminder that He was there "wash(ing) me, (so) I will be whiter than snow." (Psalm 51:7b)

It's in those moments of reading, reflection, remembering and prayer that God's gifts and promises will cling much like the sticky snowflakes that have draped themselves over the outstretched arms of giant trees and blanketed the grass, rocks and gardens below. In quiet moments spent with him, drinking in His peace and beauty, God reminds us that no matter the circumstances, all is right in this world; not through anything we can say or do or not say or not do, but because He is here with us and His grace is all we'll ever need. "For I am convinced that neither death nor life, neither angels nor demons, neither the present nor the future, nor any powers, neither height nor depth, nor anything else in all creation, will be able to separate us from the love of God that is in Christ Jesus our LORD." (Romans 8:38-39)

His love is beyond anything we could ever have imagined. Nothing can get in its way. We are His and He is ours and He promises us that will never change. What an incredible treasure we have in Him!

Dear Heavenly Father,
Thank You for your indescribable gifts of love, mercy and grace; for the clarity only You can provide; for meeting each one of us exactly where we need You to and for touching, healing and making us "as white as snow!"

Please be with each one of your children in each and every circumstance. Please always lift us away from evil lies and thoughts of despair; pull us into your hopeful promises, and embrace us in your loving arms.

Lord, let us reflect your love back to You and to those You have so generously placed in our lives to be "your love with skin on" and encourage us through life's challenges! They are such gifts!

Even more than these though Lord, please help us to see and be merciful toward those who feel invisible; and the undesirable or difficult people in our lives. Let us shine your light and love into the lives of those who are broken, hurting and alone so that all would come to know how loving, merciful and gracious You are and how valuable and loved they are because of You!
In Jesus Holy, Precious and Beautiful Name!
Amen.

Rejoicing and Persevering in Prayer

Mighty Giants; Cathedral Grove, Vancouver Island, British Columbia

© Bob Crosby

This shot was taken in the midst of Cathedral Grove; a gorgeous old growth forest that the lumber company, MacMillan Bloedel donated to the province. It simply reminded me that looking straight up always improves one's outlook! "For it is by grace you have been saved, through faith-and this is not from yourselves, it is the gift of God - not by works, so that no one can boast. For we are God's handiwork, created in Christ Jesus to do good works, which God prepared in advance for us to do." (Ephesians 2: 8-10)

There is beauty, serenity and hope when we focus on God above and forget about the challenges below; when we remember our value comes from our relationship with God and nothing more! Like the four glass lenses needed for a pair of binoculars to improve our view, praying, persevering, reading the Bible and spending time with our faith community helps focus our attention up to magnify God's promises and presence in our lives. Below, there can be a tangled mess of roots and foliage to trip us up, along with the many muddied and muddled puddles of life; which may be why Jesus taught us to wash each other's feet. We need God, and we need each other to really thrive and become the giants God intended for us to be. With His help we can stand as tall and unshakable as the ancient trees of the rain forest; reaching out our "branches" to support other believers and non-believers with God's love and truth; and stretching up toward His SON light as it leads us on to our eternal home.

"Then Jesus told his disciples a parable to show them that they should always pray and not give up. He said: "In a certain town there was a judge who neither feared God nor cared about men. And there was a widow in that town who kept coming to him with the plea, 'Grant me justice against my adversary.' For some time he refused. But finally he said to himself, 'Even though I don't fear God or care about men, yet because this widow keeps bothering me, I will see that she gets justice, so that she won't eventually wear me out with her coming!'" (Luke 18: 1-5)

Do you find it hard to always pray and not give up? I know I often do and if it weren't for remembering the times God met me in the past and how much I need Him, I'm pretty sure there are prayers I still utter now that I would have given up on years ago. The thing is though; I don't want to be responsible for letting go of someone. Who knows when maybe that one last prayer might open the floodgates to salvation and/or free them from physical, mental or spiritual suffering?

Adrianne (affectionately known as Adie,) my dear sister in Christ, who also happens to be my co-author and illustrator of our first book project, knows what it's like to keep praying. It took a long time to rise above life's circumstances but now Adie radiates God's love, light and the life she lives "treading" on His "heights." Adie had a difficult life. Her father, a doctor from Scotland, died when she was very young. Her mother, broken and reeling turned to the bottle and her children suffered from hunger and neglect. After a life of plenty, they landed in one of the poorest parts of London and Adie and her sisters struggled with their mom's liquor induced anger. It was nothing for her to rouse them in the middle of the night and insist they clean their flat. Hunger, fatigue and dyslexia ensured a difficult time in school. At the age of 15 Adie's mother passed away. Things were bleak; Adie would have to go live in an orphanage if it weren't for her older brother who offered to become her guardian. He sent for her to come and live with him and his wife in Canada.

Always up for an adventure, Adie still faced the sorrow of leaving the rest of her family and friends behind. In Canada she met and married her husband Brian. They had two sons and Adie took herself off to night school so she could learn to read them a bedtime story. Later she went to college and became a nursing assistant. It seemed that life was getting better. However, Adie's married life did not live up to the promises. Brian was a big hearted, kind man without a mean streak in his body but he suffered from depression and withdrew from Adie and the children. Adie, working full time to pay the bills, trying to raise her two sons and care for her husband and in-laws, was overwhelmed and exhausted. She became quite ill. Eventually Adie was diagnosed with Multiple Sclerosis; another blow and a subsequent loss of income.

After years of enduring and with her sons grown up, she just couldn't do it anymore. Adie left Brian and started a new life on her own. Living off her small disability allowance, she still managed, never wavered in her faith in God, trusted Him for her provision and continued to be generous with the people around her, sharing what she had. God blessed her.

Here's what I really want to talk about though; the power of prayer. Some of you may have been hurt and find this offensive. I was dreadfully afraid that Adie would too, but I felt a need to share with her. I was praying for her and Brian to be together again. At first when I told her, Adie just got very quiet. I was so fearful that I had hurt her; I was trying to be sensitive to the situation but it just came bubbling out. I don't remember the exact words but it was something along the lines of "Oh Adie, I hope this doesn't offend you. I'm so sorry if it does. I'm praying for you and Brian. I can just see you both back together again."

Adie laughs about it now. She tells me at first she thought: *Why are you doing this to me? Why go back, be punished and suffer more! You have no idea! But* "Somewhere along the way," Adie says, "the Holy Spirit told me to shut up and listen. I trusted that you saw something that I couldn't see."

So many times the idea of Brian and Adie together again all seemed impossible but still pressing me for prayer. I can't say I prayed every day but whenever it came to mind, I would pray for a restoration for Brian and Adie. Many years went by. At some point, Brian became very ill, filled with fluid until his feet and legs were open and festering. Brian was unable to get himself up even to go to the washroom and he was living alone trapped in his chair.

When Adie first saw Brian she was shocked. God sure knew what He was doing when He made her a nurse! Adie got in there like Jesus washing His disciple's feet; "Jesus knew that the Father had put all things under his power, and that he had come from God and was returning to God; so he got up from the meal, took off his outer clothing, and wrapped a towel around his waist. After that, he poured water into a basin and began to wash his disciples' feet, drying them with the towel that was wrapped around him." (John 13:3-5)

Adie worked tirelessly to care for Brian's wounds and clean up the mess around him. She also started a campaign with doctors and the health care system that lasted for years. Now Adie serves on a board trying to bring compassion into health care and ensure no one has to go through what Brian went through. Adie was also accepted for a course designed to bring humanity and caring into the medical field and support the medical staff so they will better be able to support their patients. Her faith continues to guide and give her strength.

"When he had finished washing their feet, he put on his clothes and returned to his place. "Do you understand what I have done for you?" he asked them. "You call me 'Teacher' and 'Lord,' and rightly so, for that is what I am. Now that I, your Lord and Teacher, have washed your feet, you also should wash one another's feet. I have set you an example that you should do as I have done for you."(John 13:12-15) Jesus' lesson did not go unnoticed. Adie continued to look after Brian and fight for his proper care. Brian had become obese over the years and was often chastised or ignored by medical staff. Gradually Adie was spending more and more time with her former husband. For six months she was driving to his apartment twice a day to look after him.

God has a way of answering prayers and miraculously turning the impossible into reality. At some point, despite negative responses from many, Adie decided she wanted to have Brian move back into her house with her. She knew he was dying and she wanted whatever time he had left to be positive. Talking it over with Brian, the two of them decided July would be the best time for his move. At some point though, Adie just knew it was time and moved the date up to May. God's timing, however inconvenient it might seem to us, is always perfect!

Brian moved in and they had three treasured years together before God took him home. Along the way, God provided the means for Adie to purchase a new car that was big enough for Brian to get into and they went on a wonderful road trip to show Brian Rock Creek, British Columbia, a place that has become very special to Adie. Adie glows when she speaks of Brian's last years with her. She says that "in the end, we had such a beautiful, pure, real agape love for each other."

I'm so grateful that I kept praying even when I feared it was an unpopular thing for me to be doing. I'm not saying we should pray for restoration for every marriage. I'm especially not saying that Adrianne shouldn't have left their marriage when she did. I believe it was the right thing for her then; she needed to care for her health and heart.

What I want to say is that when God presses a prayer into our hearts and minds we should obediently be in prayer with Him, even if it seems impossible. I marvel at the thought that though God doesn't need us, He gives us the exquisite joy of being able to come alongside His will and stand with Him in prayer against the enemy's lies. We don't ever have to feel weak, ineffective or hopeless in any circumstance. On our own we are; it's true, but not at all when God is with us and we are listening and relying on His power, sovereignty and the great hope we have in His name! He equips us to assist Him in the battle regardless of who we are, where we have come from or how physically, mentally, emotionally or spiritually well we are. Is it well with your soul? He wants it to be and He will make it well if you let Him.

Adie has been blessed beyond what she could have imagined and is now living her dream in her new home in Rock Creek. Here again is another testimony to the value of waiting on God and persevering in prayer. Adie wanted to move to Rock Creek years earlier. She tried valiantly and had numerous doors closed so decided she wasn't meant to go. God had her wait because He knew the best was yet to come. By obediently choosing to stay back at her home on the coast God was able to bring Adie into a close relationship with her neighbour Noris; a man who loves and encourages her. Together they bought their dream home high above Rock Creek on a mountain where Adie feels completely blessed and able to pursue her God given creative talents!

Holy Father,

I'm so grateful to be your child; loved, guided, equipped and protected by You! Help me always to rejoice and persevere in prayer with faith that You do answer and will answer with your very best no matter the circumstances!

Thank You that as Adie says "We don't have to work at miracles; they're just there, like friends." Thank You for the miracles of love You shower down on us every day and especially for your gift of grace that offers salvation to all!

Please give us all eyes to see your miracles, hearts and minds that are open to your calling and a willingness to "wash the feet" of others, even when they are covered in the muck of life's uglier realities. Help us, as You advise us in Romans 12:21 to "overcome evil with good!" Thank You for all the times You have overcome our evil with YOUR GOOD, especially on the cross! Thank You for your gift of life and love!

In Jesus Precious Name.

Amen.

Battling to See God's Blessings When My Blinders are on

Jordan River, Israel © Bob Crosby

This is *The* River; the River Jordan where Jesus himself went to be baptized by John! Likely, a scruffy group of people stood to witness the baptism; some believers, some curious onlookers, all quiet as John submerged Jesus. Imagine their shock when the voice of God rumbled out His proclamation "This is my Son with Whom I am well pleased!" (Matthew 3:17) Did any of them doubt? *...No, it couldn't be, must have been a crack of thunder. We're just getting carried away. It's all purely coincidence....nothing real about that voice....;* while others simply stood in awe of the truth that changed the world; Jesus the Messiah had arrived; God's own Son, come "to seek and save the lost!"

Looking at the ragged group gathered by the silty river bed, others may have thought *what a pathetic group of losers. I wouldn't waste my time on them! And who's this John the Baptist anyway? Why are all these people following him? For Heaven's sake, the man is clothed in dirty old camel's hair, sure he's got a leather belt but it doesn't have a designer label and the man eats locusts and wild honey! Yeah it's organic but still... If Jesus really were the son of God surely he wouldn't hang out with a guy like John!* (Or any of us for that matter...)

The good news is Jesus did and Jesus does! The things this world values don't matter to Him. You Do! This isn't because you're beautiful, wealthy, talented, athletic, clever, hardworking, productive, and exceptional or have any other spectacular traits. Jesus isn't really impressed by any of it, because if you're fortunate to have any such traits, He gave them to you anyway and only so you could use such gifts to bring Him glory - not to impress Him or others. No, Jesus cares about you because He loves you; you are His, created in God's image to love and be loved by Him. He sees you through His eyes and you are beautiful! He wants to hang out with you wherever you happen to be!

Let me say it again and not just for you but for me too. Sometimes it's too easy to forget. God only cares about YOU and your heart for him! He created you to be in a loving relationship with Him! In His perfection God can't accept any kind of sin or wrongdoing. Sadly evil exists in this world and would drive us from the love of God. So God in His great love and mercy put His plan for our saving grace into motion: "For God so loved the world that he gave his one and only Son, that whoever believes in him shall not perish but have eternal life." (John 3:16)

The sins of the world could not go unpunished by our righteous God. So it was that because of His deep love for us, God offered up His only son, Jesus Christ, to pay the price for all our sins. Did you know that? It was not for just a few, not just for some, not just for perfect people but for ALL of US! Since God is just, we had to be punished. "For all have sinned and fall short of the glory of God, and all are justified freely by his grace through the redemption that came by Christ Jesus." (Romans 3:23-24)

Since Jesus loves us, He sacrificed himself to take on the sin burden of each and every one of us. To make us right with God, Jesus was convicted and handed a death sentence for the punishment of our sins, not His! He was crucified and died on a Roman cross, was buried in a cave and on the third day, rose again victoriously. Jesus conquered death for each of us and now sits beside our God in the Heavenly realms, ready and joyfully willing to take us to Him when our time comes! We only need to believe in Him, seek His forgiveness for any wrongdoing and ask Him to be our Saviour. Then, when we confess our sin and ask Him to take us in, as Jesus said so long ago on the cross, "It is finished." We are His, assured of a "room" in His eternal "mansion," and free from guilt, pain, tears and suffering when He eventually calls us home to be with Him.

Meanwhile, we live each day on this Earth, with renewed, ludicrous hope and joy even in the face of seemingly insurmountable trials. We can enjoy the unimaginable level of peace that only Jesus can give regardless of circumstances, through the power of His Holy Spirit, who stays with us here below to strengthen, guide and intercede for us.

Will we always be joyful and peaceful in God's care here on Earth? If you're at all like me it's not likely. Sorrows creep in. Life happens and evil exists, we mess up and make poor choices. Our faith wavers. It's part of our human broken condition, but I can say without a doubt that when you make the effort to draw near to God, He will never let you down! He is the Victor in the battle and as soon as we're ready and willing He picks up every one of our broken pieces!

The Bible clearly says "Therefore God exalted Him to the highest place and gave Him the name that is above every name, that at the name of Jesus every knee should bow, in heaven and on earth and under the earth, and every tongue acknowledge that Jesus Christ is LORD, to the glory of God the Father." (Philippians 2:9-11) Ultimately we will all experience God's very Presence with His incredible love, joy, peace, mercy and grace all wrapped up in the most amazing gift this world has ever known!

I always hope that when confronted by His glory even the most stubborn atheists will come to a place where they choose God. However, love would not be love if it was forced on us and since God gave us freedom of choice, it is entirely up to each of us whether we want to meet Him later or whether we choose to "seek" Him now, "find," "ask" and experience the blessing and wonders that God's presence will "give" each one of us throughout our daily lives on this Earth.

I am so grateful for the blessings that God has showered on me and the ones I love! I wish everyone could experience that for themselves. I can't imagine doing this life without God. There are so many lonely, hurting, struggling and broken people out there trying to cope on their own strength. I only know because I was one of them. My fervent prayer is that all will come to accept Jesus as their Lord and Saviour so that they too can experience the love, peace, comfort, joy, hope and deep sense of belonging that come from Him alone!

Still, it is not my job to convert others, nor is it anyone else's. We are not to judge or rail at those who don't share our faith or culture, or those who's ideologies or identities differ from our own. Jesus never condemned, nor should we! As Christians, our job is just to remember what Jesus has done for us and let others know about Him; who Jesus is and how much He loves them!

We are simply to reflect the love and forgiveness Jesus has given ALL of us. It is my hope that at least some of this book might do just that. Please overlook my use of "many words." I've long appreciated the wise and caring words attributed to St. Francis of Assisi, "preach the gospel at all times and if necessary use words." When I/we, by the power of the Holy Spirit, choose to let go of self, put the love of God into action and place others' needs before our own we are more than able to preach the gospel without words and God will not waste that effort.

Some people claim they can't believe in God because of the suffering and evil in the world. I can't believe there could be no God because of the sacrificial love in this world! It doesn't come naturally, especially for the difficult people in our midst; and it makes no sense given our human tendency towards stubborn self-serving behaviours. It can only be because God revealed what love really is; sacrificing Himself to save the world and leaving us with the Holy Spirit to empower and equip us to live out His love!

I met an elderly rural Chinese woman once who, along with a few other ladies, spent much of her time walking over the steep karst mountain paths of Guangxi province to bring the Gospel message to people she didn't know. I've forgotten her name but she was a case study in God's sacrificial love. Through an interpreter we learned her husband had had an affair and impregnated a young woman. This older, devoted Christian lady not only forgave them; she welcomed the young woman into her home to care for her during the pregnancy and was attempting to save the funds to help the young mother eventually leave and go back to her family. Though I would like to be that gracious, I can't imagine being successful given such circumstances. I can only imagine it was by the immeasurable, unending power of God that this sweet lady was able to so beautifully and sacrificially reflect His love and light from within her being to two people who had betrayed and wronged her so badly. She let go of her "self" to become like Jesus; who despite being betrayed and wronged was so willing to love and forgive!

The Gospel message is God's love letter to the Human race. When we truly love Him, we can't help but want to love others, even when their behaviour is less than loveable; but we couldn't possibly have the strength to do it on our own. Only with prayer and by God's grace can we hope to at least partially convey God's love and mercy. God can and will take care of the rest!

I also believe, hope and trust that even when I don't see God at work, He is steadily moving mountains and winning battles for the souls he wants to welcome home eternally to His Kingdom. Mysteriously, by our prayers we are able to join with God as He unleashes His power to help others and move towards that blessed day when Christ will return and all will be made right!

I started this book pre-pandemic. It was before we ever heard of or thought about COVID-19, social distancing, self-isolation, PPE or masks. In a few short months, the virus has taken a toll on millions around the world. People are still getting sick. Many are dying and until very recently there was still no vaccine or known cure. This is not the first time, nor will it be the last time that mankind has suffered a crises, unless of course Jesus reappears before the next big crises hits and that would be just fine too!

One way or the other there is hope! God is still in control and in the end this will all come out exactly as He plans for it to. I don't believe God caused the pandemic, but I do believe that He will take this evil and turn it into something remarkably good! Perhaps this will be a catalyst that is so desperately needed to start a revival and turn more people away from worldly thinking and back to searching for God. In the Old Testament of the Bible disobedience led to some terrible things happening to His people before God's love and mercy stepped in and great good ensued. Whenever the people turned to God, He always made it right!

While we can and should take precautions to care for ourselves and others, if we are to be effective in our service we must also recognize and acknowledge we are nothing without Him. Such total reliance on God brings freedom and comfort since we can trust that we are all in His most capable, loving hands and we will get through this in the same way we always have; not on our own strength but in prayer and submission to our Heavenly Father.

When, in faith, we rely on His strength alone, God shelters us from the storm of our worldly circumstances. Under His protective wings we find rest in His love, provision, care and blessing. "He will cover you with his feathers, and under His wings you will find refuge; His faithfulness will be your shield and rampart." (Psalm 91:4) We nestle in; assured we are forgiven and knowing we are exactly where we belong; together with our Heavenly Father, Lord and Saviour and under the watchful care of the Holy Spirit, loving and interceding for us! We can trust all God's promises and know He is near.

"Though the fig tree does not bud and there are no grapes on the vines,
though the olive crop fails and the fields produce no food,
though there are no sheep in the pen and no cattle in the stalls,
yet I will rejoice in the Lord, I will be joyful in God my Savior.
The Sovereign Lord is my strength; He makes my feet like the feet of a deer,
He enables me to tread on the heights."
(Habakkuk 3:17-19)

Have you ever felt that utterly depleted yet still able to rejoice in the Lord? As the prophet Habakkuk so beautifully states, only the strength of God could ever lift us out of deep personal sorrow and need and bring us to "tread on the heights."

I have some very dear sisters in Christ from Saanich Community Church who, though I wasn't part of their church, welcomed me weekly for fellowship and Bible study whenever I was able to attend. These ladies prayerfully stood by me through times of upheaval in my life. They comforted and prayed with and for me when I first moved to Victoria and was reeling with the grief of my mother's untimely death and leaving my family and friends in Calgary. It was one of the darkest times of my life and they supported me through it all.

Then, about two years later, I contracted Lyme disease. I was ill for months and I am so grateful that my precious "family in Christ" never gave up praying for me. There were others too; family members and friends who were upholding me in prayer and with encouraging phone calls or visits; my previous church family from Northwest Community Church in Calgary, and dear "sisters" from an earlier move to Surrey B.C. who I'd met at Parkland Fellowship. I was so loved and so prayed for, yet I couldn't hold onto that. I tried desperately to pray but there were many days when I couldn't cling to God; I wasn't even sure if He was still there for me. His word still comforted me at times but I felt so distant from Him and just kept praying that I would not lose my faith. I once listened to an interview with a well-known Christian evangelist who had denounced his faith. I can still hear the interviewer ask him if he missed it. "No, I don't miss my faith but I do miss Jesus." My heart ached for him at the time and he is another one who I prayed for over the years whenever God brought him to mind. Until I was writing this, He hasn't been brought to mind for a very long time. I hope he made it back.

This became one of my deepest fears; that I would lose my faith. Sometimes it is too easy for me to question. As I sunk into my loss of strength, extreme fatigue and times of intense physical pain, my self-pity and questions were, I was afraid, leading me farther and farther from God. I was so low and so wanting it all to end that I also felt overcome with guilt; how could I feel sorry for myself when God had done so much for me! I decided I would try to keep a blessing journal. Perhaps that would pull me out of the darkness and closer to God.

Since there were days when the illness kept me pretty much confined to my bed, I kept the blessing journal and pen within arm's reach on my bedside table. My goal was to write about my blessings daily. I must confess there were days when I absolutely didn't feel like tackling it; *I'm sorry God, I just don't feel very blessed today! I'm tired of being sick and I'm sick of being tired! I just want it all to be over!*

Three things happened. First, for every day I felt that way, I'd have a little pity party, arguing with myself and God *if He was really there and truly listening*, and then I'd I just put my pen in my hand and start. There had to be something I was grateful for. I was grateful for my family, I was grateful for the sunshine out my window, I was grateful for the birds I could see in the trees, for the food I had to eat, for my husband's support… and once I started, there was more, and more and before I knew it I had a page full of blessings and barely room enough to squeeze in the last one. They were cascading out from the centre; up and down the margins, filling the page completely. Truthfully, it didn't take my pain away but it helped me remember that even though it didn't seem like it at the time, God still loved me. He was looking after me and at least I could find things to be thankful for.

Secondly, God had put all the right people in my life, praying for me without giving up and leading me to help. One of the ladies in my Saanich Community Church group had a thought. "Debbie your symptoms sound just like those of another friend of mine and he got help from a doctor in Vancouver." She got his name for me, arrangements were made and my husband Bob took me over to meet with the doctor, who immediately diagnosed it as Lyme disease and got me on antibiotics. Since I'd been sick for so many months it was unclear as to whether I could make a full recovery but again strong prayers were being lifted.

Finally, I was feeling a bit stronger and was able to attend the Bible study one Tuesday morning. I've always believed in the value of the scriptural advice that says "Is anyone among you sick? Let them call the elders of the church to pray over them and anoint them with oil in the name of the Lord. And the prayer offered in faith will make the sick person well; the Lord will raise them up." (James 5:14-16) One of my dear sister's, Grace, together with the others lifted a powerful prayer filled with the conviction of faith for healing over me and I was made well!

I'm sad that this doesn't happen for everyone. There are so many I've prayed God's healing for, fully believing they would be made well. Though some were made miraculously well, others have suffered before they were taken home to be with our Lord. This is always difficult to understand but I have found comfort in remembering God's promise, "And the God of all grace, who called you to his eternal glory in Christ, after you have suffered a little while, will Himself restore you and make you strong, firm and steadfast. To Him be the power for ever and ever. Amen." (1 Peter 5:10-14)

In 1999, when I first moved to Calgary I met another dear friend, Marilyn. As God so often does, He made us "family." Marilyn is another believing sister who is so much closer than a friend! We have shared life with all its joy and tears over the years. One of the heartaches that I shared with Marilyn was for her daughter Kimberly's physical challenges. I am ashamed to say that when I first met Kimberly, she made me uncomfortable. Unlike my daughter who is happy to engage in conversation on just about any topic, Kimberly was a victim of Cerebral Palsy, confined to a wheelchair and unable to express herself verbally. I felt inadequate, was at a loss as to how to communicate with her and would struggle to keep calm every time I witnessed one of her seizures. Her mother though, was as calm as a rock and her eyes never lost their sparkle as she lovingly cared for her daughter. Kimberly's father Jim was also devoted to giving Kimberly the best life she could have, and with her parents and brother Craig in her court, she absolutely did.

On one particular day, David Thiaw, a wonderful musician, dancer, storyteller and educator from Africa had been teaching and entertaining the students at Kimberly's school; Wilma Hansen Junior High in Calgary. When he visited Kimberly's class, the magic began. Taking her wheelchair, he brought Kimberly up to the front of the class, gently lifted her tiny hands and led them to beat out a rhythm on one of his African drums. David announced to the class, "You know she's no different than you or I. A wing is still a wing even if it is broken."

I was blessed that day to be at Kimberly's home after school. My daughter and I were taking a sewing class with Marilyn and, as often, Kimberly was stretched out on the sofa in a corner of the room. Today though, was different. When I went over to greet her, she did not look vacant.

Instead there was this unabashed, sheer light and joy filling her dainty face. Her lips were curled up in a smile and her eyes were brighter than prairie sunshine. She was the most beautiful, radiant little angel I'd ever seen.

"Kimberly, you look so happy, did you have a good day at school?" I asked knowing there could be no verbal reply. There didn't need to be. The expression on her face defied any notion that Kimberly could not express herself and left a glow that I still carry with me. Marilyn explained that David Thiaw had been visiting the school and what he had done.

Though I don't know for sure, I think in that brief moment with Kimberly, David had managed to express for her things that she had never been able to say to me nor to her classmates. Things like: *Acknowledge me. Talk to me, even when I don't answer. Include me. I'm no different than you. I have feelings too.*

I also like to think that when David Thiaw took her hands and shared that God given human connection, Kimberly's wings took flight and she soared with a new sense of freedom; the kind of freedom that can only come when it is wrapped up in love and understanding; God's kind of freedom that lets everyone know that they are welcome and they belong.

Kimberly went home to be with the Lord a number of years ago. It was a bittersweet day when we gathered to say goodbye to her broken body and celebrated Kimberly's precious life; the many lives she'd touched and the wonderful healing for her beyond our planet. Kimberly was finally free and complete in Christ.

God is our only source of love and freedom and He pours it out generously through loving hearts that are ready and willing to see others the way He sees them. Kimberly was only able to look and listen but more than able to shine God's love light into the lives of just about everyone who ever met her. All our prayers for healing weren't answered during Kimberly's earthly lifetime but she was, as her mother mentioned recently, "probably closer to God than any of us because all she could do was listen." Kimberly was a vital part of her family and community and made our little corner of the world a gentler place just by being in it. It was hard to see her suffer "for a little while," but so good to know that God "Himself" had kept His promise to "restore" Kimberly and "make *her* strong, firm and steadfast. To Him be the power for ever and ever." (1Peter 5: 10-11)

Helen, another dear "sister" in Christ has also gone through a very sad and difficult time. Just this week, we celebrated the life of her dear husband Stan who faced his trial with A.L.S. bravely and without wavering in his deep conviction of God's love. In one brief visit and through the testimony of others I can confidently say Stan's smile was as big as the ocean he liked to sail on or sit by, and his love for others moved him to many sacrificial acts of kindness. Stan absorbed

God's love daily; moment by moment and then reflected it back to those fortunate enough to spend time with him; just the way Jesus teaches us all to do.

I'd like to be as brave as Helen's husband in the face of such a horrific illness. I'm quite sure I couldn't possibly on my own strength, but Stan knew what was needed and he never failed to look to God. I hope in all our trials we will be able to do the same.

Miraculous healing on this planet within our lifetime brings unbelievable joy and I will forever be grateful for each time that happens. Still, when our best prayers for healing seem to fail, it helps me a little to remember that this is only a taste of what is to come. Praise God we will experience God's miraculous healing and even more miraculous welcoming of us into His loving presence! By the blood of Christ and His redemptive, gracious, loving power He will make us perfectly "new;" we will be free from any pain, sorrow, sin and guilt! There is no condemnation and no denying the truth; we are His and will be free to behold Him in all His glory! For my dear parents and the other loved ones who have gone before; though I miss them so much it hurts, I would never wish them back. I'm just grateful that they are residing in perfect love, peace and joy and trust they will be there to meet me.

Dear Heavenly Father,

We know that without You, we are weak and ill- equipped for the trials we face. By your power, Lord, lead us to "tread on your heights "even when things look bleak, and continue to pray with faith "being confident of this, that (You) who began a good work in (us) will carry it on to completion until the day of Christ Jesus. (Philippians 1:6) Please help us to remain faithful, recognizing your light and love and reflecting it back to others throughout our earthly lifetime. Help us to see and not to miss the miracles you provide for us daily and be grateful for each one.

Lord, please let the people around us see your light within us and be drawn to your love. Make us bold yet gentle; always willing and ready to meet others the same way You did when you walked on this Earth; on their terms, whoever they happen to be, whatever they happen to be doing and wherever they happen to be in their life journey.

We are no different than the rest; we truly are all sinners, yet You were willing to meet with us before we cleaned ourselves up! We couldn't have if we'd tried Lord; we needed You then and still need You now! Thank you for forgiving us on the cross, revealing yourself to us, and teaching us that we have been forgiven and our sins are "washed whiter than snow." Make us kind, respectful, compassionate, able, ready and willing to share the reason for our hope and our faith in You!

Finally Lord, in the beautiful words of my friend's late husband Stan; "I'm thankful for the blessings and miracles that have been bestowed upon us every day and every moment. Please go with us and before us to prepare the way and to keep us safe. Please lead the way and help us to follow."

In Jesus Precious and Holy Name!

Amen.

The End

and God willing a new beginning

So, may I leave you with this one important question?

What will YOU bring the King this year?

All God really wants is your heart! Once you give it to Him, He'll reveal where to go next.

Wishing you Love, Peace and Joy filled Journeys with Your King!

P.S. Just to clarify, where I've spoken of events as happening "yesterday," "today" or "this week" that was true of when this devotional was first penned and not at all related to the final manuscript and date of publication. Two years, several drafts, many not so "final" manuscripts and countless prayers later, this book is, God willing, ready to launch. Praying it will be a blessing of encouragement and bring honour, praise and glory to our Heavenly Father, Precious Saviour Jesus Christ and ever present Holy Spirit!

"Praise God from Whom all blessings flow; Praise Him all creatures here below, Praise Him above ye heavenly host, Praise Father, Son and Holy Ghost!" Amen.
(Doxology, Thomas Ken)

About the Photographer and the Author (Bob and Debbie Crosby)

Bob Crosby is not a professional photographer although for him photography is a serious hobby. Over the past 35 years he has sold photographs online or through direct sales over 500 times. Customers have included Reader's Digest™, Teldon Calendars™, Travel-Holiday magazine™, The Postcard Factory™, The Royal Canadian Geographical Society™, and Beautiful British Columbia Magazine™. Some of the photos in this book were taken with a Minolta SLR using slide film and scanned with a Nikon Coolscan V ED professional scanner and others with a Nikon D90 digital SLR. Bob is currently selling stock photography through iStock, a division of Getty Images. All of the images can be found at:
https://www.istockphoto.com/portfolio/bobwc?assettype=image&mediatype=photography

Fortunately Bob and I both share a passion for travel and have been blessed to travel across most of Canada and to a number of international destinations where Bob has always had his camera at the ready. God willing, we hope to do much more exploring!

We have been married over 40 years and have lived in Ontario, Alberta and British Columbia. Despite ourselves and by God's grace we managed to raise two incredibly kind, resilient and talented kids; and are now thoroughly enjoying being grandparents to two very precious grandkids! We look forward to camping trips and visits with them whenever we get the chance.

In 2018 we retired from Victoria to Nanaimo, B.C., also on Vancouver Island, where we cherish our walks by the ocean. We enjoy various projects, hobbies and organizations including Hammond Bay Baptist Church, the Nanaimo Concert Band and Nanaimo North Probus Club. Bob still does some contract work as an engineer for Ocean Networks Canada, analyzing earthquake data, contributing to their earthquake early warning system and providing outreach as a guest speaker for many schools and clubs.

I never had the career I'd hoped for, but God opened wonderful doors I never imagined. I worked as a teacher in all three provinces and had the pleasure of teaching students from preschool, elementary, junior high, and high school levels. Later, I went back to school and trained to teach English as a Second Language. This enabled me to work with many incredible adult immigrants. What a blessing it was! A variety of other jobs rounded out my working years. Two favourites were working for the Gananoque Boat Line on tours of the Thousand Islands in the St. Lawrence River and in the gift shop for the Butchart Gardens in Victoria. Every job came with trials but every experience was rich and I am so grateful for them all! I have wonderful memories of those years; especially my students, my colleagues and the tourists I met!

Now, I mostly just write, "zoom," walk, garden or try to learn and play my music; and I can't wait to be able to host and hug our visitors when the pandemic is over!

Manufactured by Amazon.ca
Bolton, ON